Hector F.E. Jungersen

The Danish Ingolf-Expedition

Vol. 3, Part 1

Hector F.E. Jungersen

The Danish Ingolf-Expedition
Vol. 3, Part 1

ISBN/EAN: 9783337723224

Printed in Europe, USA, Canada, Australia, Japan

Cover: Foto ©Andreas Hilbeck / pixelio.de

More available books at **www.hansebooks.com**

THE DANISH INGOLF-EXPEDITION.

VOLUME III.

1.

PYCNOGONIDA.

BY

FR. MEINERT.

WITH 5 PLATES AND 2 FIGURES IN THE TEXT, 1 CHART, AND A LIST OF THE STATIONS.

TRANSLATED BY TORBEN LUNDBECK.

COPENHAGEN.
BIANCO LUNO (F. DREYER), PRINTER TO THE COURT.
1899.

CONTENTS.

Pycnogonida.

	Page
Introductory remarks	1.
Terminology	1.
The History of Development	11.
Systematism	31.
I. Fam. Nymphonidæ	33.
1. Subfam. Nymphonini	34.
Gen. Nymphon (Fabr.)	34.
grossipes Fabr.	35.
Sluiteri Hoek	36.
brevitarse Kr.	37.
serratum G. O. Sars	37.
— megalops G. O. Sars	37.
Sarsii n. sp.	38.
Hoekii n. sp.	39.
Stroemii Kr.	40.
— longitarse Kr.	41.
Groenlandicum n. sp.	41.
elegans Hans.	42.
leptocheles G. O. Sars.	43.
macrum Wils.	43.
macronyx G. O. Sars	43.
— spinosum Goods	44.
— tenellum G. O. Sars	45.
robustum Bell	45.
Gen. Paranymphon Caull.	46.
spinosum Caull.	46.
2. Subfam. Pallenini	48.

	Page
Gen. Pallene (Johnst.)	48.
Pallene acus n. sp.	48.
— hastata n. sp.	49.
Gen. Cordylochele G. O. Sars	50.
— malleolata G. O. Sars	50.
— longicollis G. O. Sars	50.
Gen. Pseudopallene Wils.	50.
circularis Goods	50.
Gen. Pallenopsis Wils.	51.
— plumipes n. sp.	51.
— fluminensis Kr.	52.
II. Fam. Ascorhynchidæ	54.
Gen. Ascorhynchus G. O. Sars	55.
— tridens n. sp.	55.
III. Fam. Colossendeidæ	56.
Gen. Colossendeis Jarz.	57.
— proboscidea Sab.	57.
— clavata n. sp.	57.
— colossea Wils.	58.
— angusta G. O. Sars.	59.
macerrima Wils.	60.
IV. Fam. Phoxichilidæ	60.
2. Subfam. Pycnogonini.	60.
Gen. Pycnogonum (Brün.)	60.
— crassirostre G. O. Sars	61.
List of Literature	62.
Explanation of the Plates	65.

Pycnogonida.

By

Fr. Meinert.

The species represented in the following treatise have, with the exception of one only, been all taken on the Ingolf -expedition. The said one species is *Pallenopsis fluminensis Kr.*, which has been included in order to elucidate the genus, and throw light on this much disputed species, the original of which is still found at the Zoological Museum. The material for the developmental history has likewise mostly been taken on the said expedition, although some few species have been taken from earlier collections. The number of species taken on the Ingolf -expedition is 31, of which 8 are new to science. When 43 species are drawn and described by G. O. Sars in Den norske Nordhavs-Expedition, 1876--78 , it is to be remembered that only 20 out of these 43 species are due to the collections of the expedition.

Terminology.

Although the terminology of a group of animals chiefly depends on the systematic position of the group, and the homologies and analogies founded on this position, on the other hand it will be necessary to begin with definite appellations for each of the organs, though these appellations can only be justified by the later examination and the systematic position founded thereon. I therefore shall begin with giving a list of the names I have chosen; and as I here chiefly follow the appellations given by Sars, so I also take the liberty to copy his figure, Pycnogonidea, 1891, p. 3, which will be found on the other side.

From the two lists it will immediately be seen that I have not thought myself justified in following Dohrn, when he, more particularly after Savigny, gives to the limbs a continuous numerical order, Extremitas I VII. This way of designing the limbs has several advantages, and has also been followed by later authors, as Adlerz and Schimkéwitsch, but it has also important defects, which make themselves strongly felt. It is an advantage of the terminology of Dohrn that it is independent of all systematism; to this terminology it is all the same, whether the Pycnogonida are Crustacea or Arachnida; it has not to be altered to-day, that to-morrow, when another systematic taste is ruling, it may return to the expressions of yesterday, more or less altered in the interval. It is, however, inconvenient, when one or more of the seven pairs of limbs (extremities) are specially cr cteristic in contradistinction to the others, or when one or more pairs have disappeared, so that Extrem IV is to be understood, now as the first, now as the second, third, or fourth pair of the preserved limbs of the imago. The greatest drawback by Dohrn's way of designation is to me that it does not at all agree with the developmental history, the embryonal legs (fig. 2 b, c) not being included, and although they are not to be regarded as the predecessors of the two foremost pairs of ambulatory legs (Kroyer), they are neither the predecessors of the second and third typical pairs of limbs of the imago, the imaginal fore-limbs, or of the palpi and the ovigerous legs. I hope that it will appear from my examination of the larval development that these two pairs of limbs are not predecessors of, or identical with, the embryonal legs, to which examination the reader is referred. Now, if the embryonal legs are neither identical with the two first pairs of ambulatory legs (Kroyer), nor with the palpi and ovigerous legs (Dohrn's Extrem. II and III), there will be typically 9, and not 7, pairs of limbs, as supposed by Dohrn and all naturalists, excepting Semper, Pycnog. und Larvenf., 1874 (who has 8 pairs). Even if it be supposed that the embryonal legs are peculiar limbs, it would, of course, be possible to use the appellation of Dohrn, the list of limbs then only being increased from VII to IX; but on the other hand it would be very untoward to be always obliged to subtract several, sometimes more than the half, from the number, which is got by adding the embry-

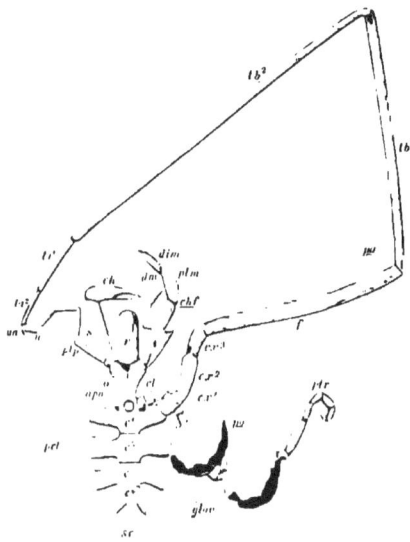

Fig. 1. Nymphon Strœmii. ♂

r.	Proboscis (rostrum).
c^1.	First segment of trunk (segmentum corporis primum).
o.	Oculiferous tubercle (tuber oculare).
cl.	Neck (collum).
apo.	Lateral process of the first segment for the insertion of the ovigerous legs (protuberantia pedis oviferi).
c^2.	Second segment of trunk (segmentum corporis secundum).
c^3.	Third segment of trunk (segmentum corporis tertium).
c^4.	Fourth segment of trunk (segmentum corporis quartum).
sc.	Caudal segment (segmentum caudale).
pcl.	Lateral process of the body for the insertion of the ambulatory legs (processus corporis lateralis).
chf.	Cheliforus (cheliforus).
s.	Scape (scapus).
ch.	Chela, or Hand (chela v. manus).
plm.	Palm (palma).
dim.	Immovable finger (acumen v. digitus immobilis).
dm.	Movable finger (pollex v. digitus mobilis).
pa.	Ambulatory legs (pes ambulatorius).
cx^1.	First coxal joint (articulus coxalis primus).
cx^2.	Second coxal joint (articulus coxalis secundus).
cx^3.	Third coxal joint (articulus coxalis tertius).
f.	Femoral joint (femur).
tb^1.	First tibial joint (articulus tibialis prior).
tb^2.	Second tibial joint (articulus tibialis alter).
ta^1.	First tarsal joint (articulus tarsalis prior).
ta^2.	Second tarsal joint (articulus tarsalis alter).
u.	Claw (unguis).
uo.	Auxiliary claw (unguiculus auxiliaris).
plp.	Palpus (palpus v. pes palpiformis).
po.	Ovigerous leg (pes ovifer).
ptr.	Terminal part of the ovigerous leg (pars terminalis pedis oviferi).
$glov$.	Egg-globe (globus ovorum).

onal legs to the pairs of limbs found in the imago. In the genus *Pycnogonum* the first pair of ambulatory legs, according to this, would be called Extrem. VI, the first five pairs of limbs having to be subtracted.

The foregoing list and figure apply to the grown larva, the young, and the imago; with regard to the young larva the following short list together with the figure of this larva, seen from the under side, must suffice.

a. Cheliforus.
b. First pair of embryonal legs.
c. Second pair of embryonal legs.
d. Proboscis.
e. First pair of ambulatory legs.
f. Second pair of ambulatory legs.

Fig. 2. *Nymphon robustum.* Larva.

I shall now proceed to notice the outer organs, giving a short description of each as well as the reason of the terms I have chosen, and at the same time I shall quote as synonyms the corresponding appellations by the chief earlier authors.

Proboscis (*rostrum*), fig. 1 r, and 2 d.

O. Fabricius: tubulus v. rostrum; Latreille: tuyau ou siphon d'une seule pièce; later (Règn. anim. éd. II): bouche; Leach: os tubulosum, or rostrum; Savigny: premier anneau du corps allongé et remplaçant la tête (vestiges de mâchoires); Johnston: rostrum; Milne-Edwards: tête; Erichson: Zunge; Kroyer: Næb (in the larva), later: Snabel (rostrum); Wilson: proboscis, or rostrum; Dohrn: Schnabel; Böhm: Rostrum; Hoek: trompe (proboscis); Adlerz: snabel; Hansen: Snabel, or Proboscis (proboscis); Sars: Snabel (proboscis), or Mundsegment.

The proboscis is the conical or almost cylindrical organ protruding from the anterior margin of the body, or from the lower side of it; it is always large or especially so in proportion to the body, and has at the point a trilobate mouth, leading to the trilateral pipe, which is closed behind by a kind of plait, protruding to a rather sharp angle and working as a filtering apparatus. The proboscis is commenced at a very early stage of the embryonal life (pl. 1, fig. 1) as a ball or tubercle without any trace of mouth, contemporary with the embryonal limbs (the chelifori and embryonal legs). It is no segment or metamere, and still less corresponding to, what in other animals is called the head, or to part of the head. Neither can it in any way be supposed to have arisen by a coalescing of gnathites.

First segment of trunk (*segmentum corporis primum*), fig. 1 c¹.

O. Fabricius: caput et thorax v. primus articulus corporis; Leach: segmentum anticum; Latreille (Règn. an. éd. II): le premier segment du tronc; Johnston: the anterior segment of thorax; Erichson: Kopf; Kroyer: Oiering og forste Brystring (annulus ocularis et annulus thoraoc is p:mus) Wilson octiferous segment; Dohrn: das erste Rumpfsegment; Bohm: Augenring; Hoek: cephalothorax; Adlerz: cephalothorax; Hansen: forste Kropring; Sars: Hovedsegment (segmentum cephalicum).

The first segment, when viewed from above, presents a simple surface without any trace of composition or articulation, and Kröyer, when he nevertheless divides it into an ocular segment and a first segment of thorax, has not been able to point out any trace of a cross-seam or any other articulation, but has evidently started from the a priori reason that eyes cannot be found on a thoracic part (cp. the following). If the animal, however, is seen from before, several seams or lines may sometimes be seen more or less distinctly, as marking the boundary of peculiar skeletal parts, originally independent, but now united with the first segment of the thorax. Thus under the fore-edge of the first segment of the trunk in *Pallenopsis plumipes* the common skeletal part (metamere) of the chelifori may be seen as a transverse band (pl. IV, fig. 3). To understand the first segment of the trunk, it is quite necessary to follow the larval development from the embryo. It will then be seen that the first and foremost chief part of the embryo is formed by the proboscis and the three pairs of embryonal limbs surrounding this latter, while the other chief part is not developed till later, the ambulatory legs and the four segments of the trunk together with the caudal segment not being partitioned off at first. The first chief part, most frequently with the exception of the chelifori, shrinks by and by, loses its independence of the other chief part, and is, as it were, swallowed up by the foremost part of this latter, the first segment of the trunk; not until this has taken place, and the embryonal legs have fallen off, do the imaginal fore-limbs, palpi and ovigerous legs, spring forth on the lower side of this segment, when they are developed at all. The further details of this growth will be found in the following in the section treating of the larval development.

If we suppose that the four segments with the ambulatory legs of the Pycnogonida correspond with the thorax of the other Arthropoda, especially with that of the Arachnida and Insects, and the first principal segment of the embryo with its three pairs of limbs likewise corresponding with the head of those animals, the name of Cephalothorax (Hoek, Adlerz) for the first segment of the trunk would be very good; but as I consider this comparison as wrong, or, at all events, as indemonstrable, I shall prefer another, less marked appellation, and as such I consider the one I have chosen. I, for my part, think it to be most probable, or at all events possible, that the second principal segment of the Pycnogonida with its four pairs of ambulatory legs and the caudal segment can be compared with the abdomen of the Arachnida, in which this part in its development has, or may have a similar division into somites, and similar rudimentary limbs as in the Pycnogonida, cp. Locy: Developm. Agelena, 1885, pl. II, fig. 9—11, and pl. III, fig. 13—15. The position of the genitals then would also, as generally is the case, be in the abdomen, and in the processes of the abdomen, that is, the ambulatory legs. On the other hand, the eyes would be placed on the fore edge of the abdomen, but eyes (and peduncles in the pedunculated Crustacea) do not form a typical part of the body in any animal, belonging to or constituting the head; and even if we, to avoid this difficulty, should call the part of the body, in which the eyes are placed, cephalothorax, it is still in the hindmost part of this segment, in the thorax, or the first somite of it that the eyes would be placed — and farther forward, to the head itself, they would never come.

The oculiferous segment of Wilson and the Augensegment of Bohm is only another expression taken from the appellation of Kroyer, but applied to the whole of the first segment of the trunk. When Erichson uses the name of Kopf for this part of the body, it is exclusively with regard to the ambulatory legs and the comparing them to the limbs of the Arachnida, of which again the three last pairs were to correspond to the thoracical legs of the Insects, while all the corresponding segments were to form the thorax.

Oculiferous tubercle (*tuber oculare*), fig. I, *o*.

Kroyer: Oieknude (protuberantia ocularis); Sars: Oieknude (tuberculum oculiferum).

On the dorsal side of the first segment of the trunk, in the middle of it, but more or less backward, is found a knob-like protuberance, the oculiferous tubercle. The shape of this knob is very different, varying in the different genera and species, growing from a low, rounded swelling to a height of almost the length of the trunk, and ending with a tapering point. It is not until the second larval stage of development that the oculiferous tubercle begins to be seen as an excrescence on the first segment of the trunk after this segment being distinctly separated. The eyes make their appearance prior to the oculiferous tubercle on the spot of the first segment of the trunk, from which this latter rises, and during the growth of the tubercle the eyes are raised with it more or less, so that in the imago they are placed in a square round the tubercle, more or less distant from its top. The tubercle bears typically four single eyes, ocelli, but frequently the eyes are not, or only a little, developed, so that as well blind species as seeing ones may be found in the same genus (*Colossendeis*).

Neck (*collum*), fig. I *cl*.

I have thought it best, like Sars, to keep this name for the middle part of the first thoracical segment, when it is more or less strongly marked off, as I regard this appellation as so little marked, that it is no necessary consequence to look upon or denominate as head the thickened part of the trunk lying before the segment in question.

Lateral process of the first segment for the insertion of the ovigerous legs (*protuberantia pedis oviferi*), fig. I *apo*.

Sars: Halsfortsats (processus colli) til Fæste for de falske Fodder.

This process originates from the under side of the first segment of the trunk just before the process of the trunk; it is very short, inconspicuous, and from its outer side or point arises the ovigerous leg. When the segment of the trunk is short, so that there is no neck, the palpi get towards it, and in some genera (*Colossendeis*) the palpi do apparently arise from the fore side of this process.

Second segment of trunk (*segmentum corporis secundum*), fig. I *c2*.

Third segment of trunk (*segmentum corporis tertium*), fig. I *c3*.

Fourth segment of trunk (*segmentum corporis quartum*), fig. I *c4*.

No synonyms are here necessary to explain the opinion of the authors as to these segments. It is a matter of course, and everybody agrees that they are homonomous with the first segment of trunk, or, at all events, with the large upper and hinder part of it.

Caudal segment (*segmentum caudale*), fig. I *sc*.

Linné: cauda; O. Fabricius: cauda; Latreille: le dernier segment du corps; Lamarck: abdomen; Leach: abdomen; Savigny: abdomen; Johnston: abdomen; Milne-Edwards: abdomen; Erichson: Hinterleib; Kröyer: Bagkrop, abdomen; Wilson: abdomen; Dohrn: Hinterleib; Böhm: Abdomen; Hoek: abdomen; Adlerz: abdomen; Hansen: Bagkrop (abdomen); Sars: Haleségment (segmentum caudale).

The appellation of this part of the trunk was in the early authors (Linné and O. Fabricius) simply cauda, tail; but Latreille having pointed out that it was a part, a segment, of the trunk itself, the first name was displaced by the appellation abdomen and the translations of it (Hinterleib, Bagkrop), which was adopted by all authors until Sars, the opinion being, I suppose, that it corresponded to the abdomen of the other Arthropoda, especially that of the Insects and the Arachnida. Sars, as it were, has meant to adopt the old name of tail, but on account of the prevalent aversion to this appellation, he has altered it to the mediate one of caudal segment, and I have followed him partly of similar reasons.   As to its development the caudal segment is the hindmost part of the hindmost principal division of the embryo, and until a far advanced stage in the larval development it forms a hindmost, gradually more protruding, process of the fourth segment of trunk. If upon the whole it is separated from this segment by a dermal suture, this does not take place until the third larval stage. It never bears limbs, but the intestinal canal opens in the end of it with a weak squirting apparatus. Thus the caudal segment no doubt belongs to and makes the hindmost part or segment of the same principal portion to which the four preceding segments belongs; it is no separate part of the body, different from the foregoing segments of the trunk, no abdomen in contradistinction to a thoracical part, lying before it. The caudal segment can be proportionally very long, almost as long as the body, and then it is also well separated from the fourth segment of the trunk and very slender; there is no trace of division in joints, not even in Zetes (Euryeydes), as has been maintained. On the other hand this segment may also be quite small, as it were, rudimentary, as I know from a not described genus among the collections, which the Smithsonian Institute has given me for examination.

Lateral process of the body for the insertion of the ambulatory legs (processus corporis lateralis), fig. 1 pcl.

Sars: Legemets Sidefortsatser (processus laterales corporis) til Fæste for Gangfodderne.

These processes of the body and the ambulatory legs attached to them, are structures characteristic of the Pycnogonida, as they are not formed by germinating or growth of a particular cellular group but, as is distinctly seen from my drawings of the embryo, by a bag-like constriction of the ectoderm, in the same manner as the embryonal limbs (the chelifori and embryonal legs). They are in reality only parts of the body, and so it will easily be understood, that the intestinal canal and the sexual glands can continue far into the ambulatory legs as processes of the body.

Cheliforus (chelitorus), fig. 1 chf and 2 a.

Linné: palpi; O. Fabricius: palpi; Latreille: mandibules; later (Règn. an. éd. II): antennepinces; Leach: mandibulæ; Savigny: pedes secundi; Lamarck: antennules; Johnston: mandibles; Milne-Edwards: pattes-mâchoires; Erichson: erstes Kieferpaar or Scherenkiefer (Mandibeln); Kröyer: Saxe (antennæ cheliformes); later Kindbakker (mandibulæ); Böhm: Kieferfühler; Wilson:

antennæ; Hoek: mandibules; Hansen: Kindbakkeantenner (antennæ mandibulares, also mandibulæ); Morgan: cheliceræ; Sars: Saxlemmer (chelifori).

The chelifori are the foremost of the three pairs of embryonal limbs, and in most Pycnogonida they grow on, and are kept to the stage of the imago. Only rarely they are thrown off during one of the larval stages (fam. *Phoxichilida* - in *Pycnogonum* already on the second larval stage, pl. 1, fig. 4), or by the last casting of the skin in the young (*Colossendeis augusta* and *gracilis*). They are often more or less rudimentary, especially in the outermost joints (*Ascorhynchidæ*). Their resemblance to the first pair of limbs in the Arachnida is conspicuous, and there can be no doubt of their importance with regard to the systematism. This consideration has also asserted itself in the appellations, used for these limbs by most authors, and when nevertheless these appellations are so different, the reason may be sought in the fact that also the foremost limbs of the Arachnida have very different names; but as I think the names of antenna, mandible, or mandible-antenna in the Arachnida to be equally objectionable, I have preferred partly after Kroyer, and together with Sars to use the appellation of cheliforus for the whole limb.

Scape (*scapus*), fig. 1 *s*.

Kroyer: Grundled (articulus basalis); Sars: Skaftet (scapus).

The cheliforus is divided into two chief parts, a basal or advancing part, and a terminal or prehensile part. Of these the former sometimes is undivided, sometimes bipartite. The bipartition is generally distinctly shown by a suture and by muscles, and but rarely it is only more or less indicated, so that it may be doubted whether the scape has one or two joints (*Pallenopsis*).

Chela or hand (*chela*), fig. 1 *ch*.

Kroyer: Sax (chela); Hansen: Tang or Sax (chela); Sars: Sax (chela).

By the appellation chela or hand is designated the second chief part of the cheliforus, and it will, on account of the systematism, be necessary to give special names to the separate parts. I have supplemented the appellation by Kroyer and Sars of the second chief part of the cheliforus by the expression hand , because the separate parts, of which it consists, are named with appellations from the hand. The chela or hand is the two outermost joints of the cheliforus, the first of which forms a proportionally broad part, sending out laterally a long tooth- or finger-shaped process, which towards the point meets with the point of the movable last joint. The hand may be more or less rudimentary, or even wholly disappear.

Palm (*palma*), fig. 1 *plm*.

Kroyer: Palmen (palma); Hansen: manus; Sars: Palmen (palma).

Immovable finger (*acumen v. digitus immobilis*), fig. 1 *dim*.

O. Fabricius: acumen; Kroyer: ubevægelig Finger (digitus immobilis); Hoek: griffe immobile des mandibules; Bohm: der unbewegliche Finger; Hansen: pollex; Sars: den ubevægelige Finger (pollex).

O. Fabricius already felt impelled to distinguish between the immovable finger of the hand and the movable outer joint of the cheliforus, and called the former acumen, instead of which expression Kroyer used immovable finger (digitus immobilis); Sars and Hansen, I think after him, next introduced the expression pollex (i. e. thumb) for this process, though this latter name had already been used by O. Fabricius and Kroyer of the last joint of the cheliforus, the movable finger.

Movable finger (pollex v. digitus mobilis), fig. 1 dm.

O. Fabricius: pollex; Kroyer: Tommel (pollex); Hoek: griffe mobile des mandibules; Wilson: dactylus; Bohm: Scheerenfinger or Daumen; Hansen: Index; Sars: bevægelige Finger (dactylus)

I have kept the old name of O. Fabricius and Kroyer pollex or movable finger for the terminal joint of the cheliforus, or the movable finger of the hand, and can see no reason to introduce instead of it the dactylus of Wilson.

To avoid every misconception it would perhaps be best to omit the use of the short names of pollex, dactylus, index, and thumb, and to abide by the appellations digitus immobilis and digitus mobilis, immovable and movable finger, as I have done in the synoptical figure by choosing the letters dim and dm.

Ambulatory leg (pes ambulatorius), fig. 1 pa and 2 e, f.

Schimkéwitsch, Pantop. Vettor Pisani, gives to the first pair of ambulatory legs also the separate name: Patte-mâchoire.

The rise and development of the four pairs of ambulatory legs follow the larval development, and they are never wanting in the imago, nor reduced in any way but at most by the defective development or the falling off of the claws or the auxiliary claws. They arise from the ends of the lateral processes of the body, and are, to judge from the rudiments in the embryo and the larva, as has been mentioned, only prolongations of these processes, constricted into the number of nine joints, inclusive of the claw, which is common to all Pycnogonida.

First coxal joint (articulus coxalis primus), fig. 1 c¹.

Second coxal joint (articulus coxalis secundus), fig. 1 c².

Third coxal joint (articulus coxalis tertius), fig. 1 c³.

Sars: 3 Hofteled (articuli coxales).

These three joints form the proximal end of the ambulatory leg; they belong to the shortest joints of the leg, and form a series of homonomous joints, being of one set; therefore they may all together correctly be termed the coxa.

Femoral joint (femur), fig. 1 f.

Sars: Laarled (articulus femoralis).

In the Arthropoda, especially the Insects, the femoral joint follows upon the coxa and coxal segment or trochanter, which in these animals is only a subordinate joint. I think it, however, impossible to transfer the terminology of the legs of the Insects to those of the Pycnogonida, and therefore I have considered it advisable to follow Sars in his appellations of the joints of the leg, only with some variation in the special names.

First tibial joint (articulus tibialis prior), fig. 1 tb¹.

Second tibial joint (articulus tibialis alter), fig. 1 tb².

Sars: Lægled (articuli tibiales).

These two joints of the leg are closely united, and there is no reason to give any prominence to either of them, and so I agree with Sars in not using unnecessary appellations, taken from the Arachnida or other Arthropoda. There is thus no reason to call one of the joints patella.

First tarsal joint (articulus tarsalis prior), fig. 1 ta¹.

Sars: Tarsalled (tarsus).

Second tarsal joint (articulus tarsalis alter), fig. 1 ta².

Sars: Fodled (propodus).

These two tarsal joints are closely united like the two tibial joints; often they are almost uniform without any particular difference as to length or structure. If there is any difference, it consists most frequently in the first joint being shortened, often much shortened in contrast to the second one. If we should choose to distinguish between the joints, and give each of them a separate name, I think that appellations as metatarsus and tarsus would be proper; but to avoid too many names and all confusion with the appellations of Sars, I have only numbered the joints. The names given by Sars, seem to me to be too unfortunate at all events; the name of tarsus meaning always the outermost joint, or — if the tarsus is divided — joints of the leg.

Claw (unguis), fig. 1 u.

Sars: Endeklo (unguis terminalis).

The claw, as mentioned above, is only the last terminal joint of the leg (corresponding to the claw in the larva of the Staphylinids and of most Coleoptera), but is not included in the foot. It is very much varying as to shape and size, often in the same genus (for inst. in Colossendeis); as it cannot be mistaken for any other claw, I have thought it unnecessary to use a more particular appellation.

Auxiliary Claws (unguiculi auxiliares), fig. 1 ua.

Sars: Bikloer (unguiculi auxiliarii).

These auxiliary claws are really the terminal claws of the foot, originating from and attached to the last joint (the claw) of the foot. In so far they are real claws, and correspond to the claws in the Arachnida and most Insects. Corresponding claws are wanting in the Crustacea, and therefore their presence in the Pycnogonida is of no small systematic importance; it is to be remarked, however, that they often become rudimentary or quite disappear, but nevertheless they may be said to be typical in this group of animals. As to their importance in assisting the claw, it evidently cannot be great, and therefore their Latin name of auxiliares or auxiliarii is not very appropriate.

Palp (palpus v. pes palpiformis), fig. 1 plp.

Linné: antennæ; O. Fabricius: antennæ; Latreille: palpes ; Leach: palpi; Savigny: pedes tertii; Lamarck: antennules; Johnston: palpi; Milne-Edwards: palpes; Erichson: zweites Kieferpaar, Maxillen, Tasten; Kroyer: Palper; later: first pair of jaws or Maxiller (maxillæ primi paris); Wilson: palpi; Bohm: Palpen; Hoek: palpes; Hansen: Palper; Sars: Foler (palpi).

After Latreille, more particularly, perhaps, founded on his theory of the proboscis being formed by a composition of gnathites, having introduced the appellation palpes for the word antenna used by Linné, this name (palpi- palpes) has now been used by almost all later authors; some (Erichson, Kroyer) have thought, however, that this pair of limbs do not correspond to the palps of the other Arthropoda only, but to the whole corresponding pair of gnathites, and have named at according to this opinion (Kiefer, Maxillen). In Dohrn, Adlerz and Schimkéwitsch it of course becomes Extrem II. As I, as well as Dohrn, reject the theory of Latreille, I have retained the name of palps.

The palps are the first pair of the imaginal fore limbs; they do not arise, until the embryonal legs have been thrown off, and have no continuous connection with the latter. They always originate from the anterior edge of the lower side of the first segment of the trunk, often at a great distance from the ovigerous legs; but when the segment is shortened they approach the ovigerous legs, even so far as to apparently originating from the lateral process, on which those legs are inserted (*Colossendeis*). It is to be supposed that they are of no great importance in the life of the animal, and they also form the pair of imaginal limbs, which are liable to the greatest changes as to length, number of joints etc., and soonest become rudimentary or are thrown off. In *Ascorhynchus tridens* I have in the fourth joint of these limbs found a particular organ of sense (?); as to details see the following section on the ovigerous legs.

Ovigerous leg (*pes ovifer*), fig. 1 *po*.

Linné: tentacula pectoris; O. Fabricius: pedes spurii (fila ovifera); Latreille: pattes; later (Règn. an. éd. II): fausses pattes; Leach: organa ovifera; Savigny: pedes quarti; Johnston: oviferous legs; Milne-Edwards: appendices pediformes; Erichson: drittes Kieferpaar; Kroyer: andet Par Kjæber, Æggetraad; Wilson: accessory legs; Böhm: Eiträger; Hoek: pattes ovifères; Hansen: pedes ovigeri; Sars: falske Fodder (pedes spurii).

The most common appellations of this second pair of imaginal fore limbs are owing to the fact that they are used for carrying the eggs. Another starting point may be found in the peculiar position of these limbs, as seemingly they can be classed neither among the gnathites nor among the ambulatory legs, a fact already pointed out by O. Fabricius.

The ovigerous legs are the latest developed limbs, even if their development takes place only a little later than that of the palps. They arise on a level with and behind the palps on a particular process, but their position in relation to the palps, especially with regard to distance, has already been mentioned. They are of a more considerable length and most frequently have more joints than the palps. The number of joints is typically ten, exclusive of the claw, that is to say, one more than the number we arrive at in the ambulatory legs, when in these we count the claw as a joint, and consider the auxiliary claws as corresponding to the claw of the ovigerous legs. Their most important function is in the male to carry the eggs, for which purpose some of the joints are often thickened or provided with particular hair-formations especially in the male. Besides I have in different species of Nymphonidæ (*Nymphon groenlandicum* n. sp. pl. III, fig. 20*a*; *Pallene hastata* n. sp. pl. IV, fig. 17*a*) and as well in the male as in the female, found in the fourth joint of these limbs an inner organ consisting of a lengthened bag, divided, as it were, into two parts by a constriction in the middle; this bag is by long ligaments of connective tissue, arising from its anterior and posterior end, attached to the exoskeleton; a broad nerve runs along the longitudinal side of the bag. No doubt this bag is an organ of sense, I suppose, of hearing. In the *Ascorhynchus* quite a similar organ is found, only that in this animal it is not found in the ovigerous legs, but in the palps (cp. above). But besides serving as bearers of the eggs in the male and bearers of an organ of sense, they serve, as I suppose, in both sexes as combs or cleansing apparatus for the other limbs of the animal, all of which can presumably be brought within the sphere of action of the rows of dermal leaves[1] (the comb) with which the last joints of the ovigerous legs are provided.

The terminal part of the ovigerous leg (*Pars terminalis pedis oviferi*), fig. 1 *ptr.*

Sars: Endeled (pars terminalis).

I have, as Sars, given a special name to these four last joints of the ovigerous leg, bearing the comb or cleansing apparatus, just mentioned. The comb consists of a greater or lesser number of daggershaped dermal leaves with deeply incised edges, arising in one or more rows from the inner side of these four joints. The claw, with which the leg terminates, is closely joined to the comb, and as it is often deeply incised in its inner edge it also partakes in the work of the comb.

The egg-globe (*globus ovorum*), fig. 1 *glov.*

Sars: Eggeklump (globa ovorum).

The male, as it is well known, (Cavanna, Studi Pienog., 1877) carries the deposited eggs, placed in lumps around one or more of the middle joints of the ovigerous legs. As the size of the eggs is very different in the different Pycnogonida, so it is also with that of the lumps, but most frequently the size of the lumps and of the eggs stands in an inverse ratio to each other. As a rare exception the males of some species carry the eggs in one cake on the lower side of the body (*Pycnogonum*), while the males of other species have some few, very large eggs attached singly to the ovigerous legs (*Pallene*). The number of egg-globes most frequently is two, one globe on each of the two legs, but frequently this number is doubled or increases further to 4—5 globes on each leg. Very rarely only one leg has one single egg-globe; I have, however, found this to be the case in by far the most of the males of *Nymphon robustum*, that I have had for examination.

The preceding survey of the limbs and parts of the body of the Pycnogonida applies also to the young larvæ, in so far as those limbs and parts have been developed; but besides these larvæ have particular limbs, and to show these limbs I have on p. 3 given a contour-drawing of such a larva, fig. 2. Especially are to be mentioned:

Embryonal leg of the first pair (*Pes embryonalis prioris paris*), fig. 2 *b.*

Embryonal leg of the second pair (*Pes embryonalis alterius paris*), fig. 2 *c.*

These two pairs of limbs develop at the same time as the chelifori (or the first pair of embryonal legs) and the proboscis on the first chief part of the embryo; they soon attain to their full development, but are also early thrown off during the second or third larval stage. Only rarely they are not developed at all (*Pallene hastata*, pl. 1, fig. 18—19) or grow only to short, tap-like processes (*Pseudopallene spinipes*, pl. 1, fig. 8, and *Pseud. circularis*, fig. 10, as well as *Pallene brevirostris*, fig. 16).

The History of Development.

On the development of the Pycnogonida there exists a rather considerable literature. The attention must first be drawn to the fact that the common distinction, also used in this work, which

[1] By Sars these leaves or blades are rather unluckily named Randtorner, in English marginal spines.

is made between the embryonal and the larval stage, cannot be fully kept up with regard to the development of the Pycnogonida. The general mark of distinction (whether the embryo has or has not left the egg) is here of only very little importance, and nearly related forms, even species of the same genus, may attain to a different, sometimes very different development in the egg. Accordingly it will not do to deny the metamorphosis in such forms as do not leave the egg until they have attained their permanent shape. This opinion and the interpretation of the larval development now generally current have been expressed by Korschelt a. Heider (1890) p. 662 seq: Die meisten Pantopoden entwickeln sich mittelst Metamorphose. Ihre Larven weisen gewöhnlich drei Extremitätenpaare auf, doch verlassen einige in höherer Ausbildung das Ei; so besitzen die jungen Pallenen[1] beim Ausschlüpfen bereits sämmtliche Extremitäten und auch einige Arten der Gattung Nymphon erreichen schon im Ei diese höhere Entwickelungsstufe. Die verschiedenen Arten der letztgenannten Gattung differiren übrigens in dieser Beziehung, da die Larven einiger beim Ausschlüpfen nur vier oder fünf Extremitätenpaare aufweisen (Hoek). As will be seen from this quotation, Korschelt and Heider found their statement especially on the examinations by Hoek, or recapitulate the principal contents of the description of Hoek as it is given in his last great work: Nouvelles études sur les Pycnogonides (1881), p. 482 seq.

But before I pass to my own representation of the developmental history I shall give a short historical view of the most important works in this branch of study, and as we have already in Dohrn: Die Pantopoden des Golfes von Neapel (1881) a very copious literary survey, I may limit myself to the following four authors: Kroyer, Dohrn, Hoek and Morgan.

Kroyer is the author to be named first, not only because he first of all has studied and described larvæ of the Pycnogonida, but also on account of his contributions being the most important ones we hitherto have got concerning the development of these animals. Already his Om Pycnogonidernes Forvandlinger (On the metamorphoses of the Pycnogonida) (1849) is of great importance, but still more so is the series of representations of larval forms given on pl. 39 of the great, unfinished French work of travel: Gaimard, Voyages en Scandinavie etc. (1849) to which never appeared any text or explanation. As such an explanation may with regard to the Pycnogonida be taken Kroyer's Contributions to our knowledge of the Pycnogonida, Bidrag til Kundskab om Pycnogoniderne eller Sospindlerne (1845). In the close of the third section of this treatise, on the metamorphoses of the Pycnogonida, l. c. p. 136 seq. Kroyer collects the laws that seem to regulate the development of the Pycnogonida under 5 principal heads which may briefly be rendered thus: 1 The Pycnogonida pass through 3 stages. 2 The first stage is of a thick, swollen shape; filled with yolk substance; without any abdomen; with a proboscis; with cheliferous Kindbakker (mandibles); and with 2 pairs of feet. Eyes seem to be wanting. 3 In the second stage a third pair of feet are found, but they are short, and have only an indistinct articulation, or none at all. Eyes as well as the first and second pair of Kjæber (maxilles) can be distinguished, at least in some species. Sometimes the yolk substance of the body is present, in which case the young one passes this stage under

---

[1] This statement does not apply to all Pallene-species. The species of this genus that I have examined, as will be seen in the following, leave the egg, when the three foremost pairs of ambulatory legs have been developed and before the rest: the fourth pair and the ovigerous legs.

the belly of the mother (the father it ought to be); sometimes the yolk is consumed, and then the young one has to find its food. 4° In the third stage the larva gets the fourth and last pair of (rudimentary) feet. The two preceding pairs (the three preceding must be meant) are very much developed. The maxillæ (i. e. palps and ovigerous legs) on the contrary, are still, in the species where they are found, quite rudimentary. 5 After a new casting of the skin the animal nearly gets its permanent shape, although the length of the body and the limbs is altered not a little.

Dohrn in a couple of works has given important contributions to the history of development, first in his: Untersuchungen über Bau und Entwickelung der Arthropoden (1870) in the second section of which, with the sub-title Ueber Entwickelung der Pycnogoniden , he treats of the development of the larva of *Pycnogonum litterale*, *Achelia lævis* and *Phoxichilidium* sp. Still more important, however, is the contribution, he has given in the monograph entitled: Die Pantopoden des Golfes von Neapel (1881), in which, besides descriptions and figures of many different genera as *Barana*, *Ammothea, Clotenia, Phoxichilus, Phoxichilidium* and *Palleue*, he gives an account of the larvæ known to him, and their development l. c. p. 69—80. The principal progress in our knowledge of the development given by Dohrn is that he justly shows how Kroyer has been wrong in his interpretation of the development of the two foremost pairs of ambulatory legs, as if those pairs had arisen by an uninterrupted development of the two hindmost pairs of limbs in the first form of the larva, the embryonal legs as I have called them. Kroyer's error is, I suppose, principally due to the fact that in the very young larva of *Palleue* (or *Pseudopalleue*) these limbs are almost or entirely wanting, and so Kroyer has taken the two foremost pairs of legs (i. e. ambulatory legs) to be corresponding to the two foremost pairs of legs (i. e. embryonal legs) in the larva of the other species. In the following I shall again recur to this subject.

The works on the Pycnogonida by Hoek are well known. The two most important are: Report on the Pycnogonida in the Voyage of H. M. S. Challenger (1881) in which he on the plates XIX and XX represents the larvæ from their earliest development; and next his Nouvelles études sur les Pycnogonides (1881) where on pl. XXX the different larvæ are represented. Besides figures of well known forms, as *Phoxichilidium*, *Ammothea* and *Pycnogonum*, he especially draws different species of the genus *Nymphon*. In the lastmentioned treatise, l. c. p. 481 seq. Hoek gives the results of his examinations in the following way: Voici en peu de mots le résultat auquel je suis arrivé: on trouve toujours, à quelques exceptions près, comme première forme larvaire, un animal avec trois paires d'extrémités, dont la première se termine en une pince et dont les deux suivantes sont formées de deux articles et se terminent par des griffes allongées (larve Protonymphon). Les deux dernières paires d'extrémités sont — comme la première paire — des appendices simples, c'est-à-dire qu'elles ne sont pas divisées en deux branches comme celles des larves Nauplius. La bouche est placée à la fin d'une excroissance de forme cylindrique ou conique, qui est implantée entre la première et la seconde paire d'appendices: cette excroissance, c'est la trompe, qui au moment de l'éclosion de la larve est toujours très courte, mais possède déjà cette forme conique ou cylindrique.

La manière dont l'animal adulte se développe de cette forme larvaire est des plus simples. Tandis que les trois appendices originaux se métamorphosent dans les trois paires d'appendices céphaliques ou disparaissent (soit une, soit deux, soit — et ceci n'arrive jamais chez les individus

après — dans les trois pattes, les segments thoraciques se développent successivement au bord posté-
rieur du corps, et aussitôt un nouveau segment formé, une paire de pattes se montre également
comme excroissances latérales de ce segment. Quand quatre paires de pattes se sont ainsi développées
aux quatre segments thoraciques (notons que l'ordre de développement des pattes correspond tout à
fait à leur rang dans le corps de l'animal adulte), l'excroissance terminale se change en un abdomen
plus ou moins rudimentaire.

Morgan has given a little series of essays on the Pycnogonida, of which especially the last
one may be mentioned, entitled: A Contribution to the Embryonalogy and Phylogeny of the Pycnogonids
(1891). In this essay Morgan gives the development of *Phoxichilidium maxillare* [= *femoratum*
Rathke?], of *Pallene empusa*, and of *Tanystylum orbiculare*. He has more than his two above mentioned predecessors paid attention to the first development of the embryo, an examination that Kroyer
did not enter upon at all, and gives furthermore a very handsome series of the developmental stages
of the larva, especially the larva of *Tanystylum*; on the other hand I do not think his representation of the larval development of *Pallene empusa* to be correct. In his introduction l. c. p. 2 Morgan
says: For many reasons the present paper attempts in no way to give a complete answer from the
embryonal side. The very great difficulties of a suitable technique had slowly to be overcome, and
the time at command prevented a detailed description of the different organs arising from the germ-
layers, so that much remains that might be done, but nevertheless his essay is a very important
advance in our knowledge of the development of these animals, as also his representation of the
structure and development of the eye in the Pycnogonida is rather exhaustive.

Passing now to my own description of the larval development I have to begin with the usual
complaint of not having had fresh material at my disposal; but on the other hand the Ingolf-Expedition has brought home so rich a material well preserved in spirit that I suppose I shall be able to
give a more detailed and continuous description of the different stages of development in the larva.
I have been able to follow the development for a shorter or longer way in a considerable number of
Pycnogonida, belonging to the different families and genera as *Nymphon grossipes, Sluiteri, elegans,
longitarse, robustum, spinosum, macronyx; Paranymphon spinosum*[1]; *Zetes (Euryeyde) hispidus; Pseudopallene circularis* and *spinipes; Pallene hastata* and *brevirostris; Phoxichilidium femoratum; Pycnogonum
littorale*, altogether 7 genera with 15 species. The species, the development of which I have most
complete, are *Nymphon grossipes, N. robustum* and *Pseudopallene circularis*, of which three species the
first and the last are those that have been particularly examined by Kroyer; but besides corrobo-
rating most of his statements and drawings (I have partly examined his original pieces) I have also
been able to increase and partly to correct some of them, which corrections especially apply to *Pseudopallene circularis*.

The segmentation, yolk-division, of the Pycnogonid ovum is complete, sometimes equal, sometimes unequal.

For the correctness of this thesis I must refer to Morgan, Contrib. Embryol., 1891, and I
have nothing to add. It is, I think, to be supposed, as Morgan does l. c. p. 23, that the difference
between equal and unequal segmentation, which latter is also continued in the difference between

[1] l. c. Pl. for 12—21 are wrongly called spinipes in stead of spinosum.

large and small yolk parts, the macromeres and micromeres of Morgan, must be of a considerable influence for the later development, and that it is connected with or proportioned to the mass of the alimentary yolk in the egg; this fact again plays a very great part in the biology of the larva, as this latter may exist without any other food, and keep enclosed in the safe egg-shell the longer, the more alimentary yolk it brings along with it. Kroyer already has referred to this reciprocal relation in his Contributions to the knowledge of the Pycnogonida (1845), comp. especially the third of the five principal heads, under which he collects the results of his examinations, l. c. p. 137, and to which I have referred at p. 12 seq.

A germinal stripe as in the other Arthropoda, especially the Insecta, is not formed. The ganglia as well as the separate pairs of limbs are formed or constricted by degrees, from before backward, and, with the exception of the three foremost ganglia and pairs of limbs, one after the other.

In the Arthropoda, especially the Insecta, the first germ of the embryo, as is well known, is distinctly seen as a smaller or broader longitudinal band, the germinal stripe, along the under side of the egg, and from this band the formation of the abdominal nerve cord and the pairs of limbs take their rise almost at the same time; besides the formations are only small, and, as far as they really are developed, they grow in size and length by a rapid multiplying, proliferation, of the cells. In the Pycnogonida, on the contrary, a germinal stripe is never found, but the whole yolk mass is immediately enclosed by a blastoderm, and all the limbs arise, if anything, from the sides of the blastoderm by a segmentation of corresponding parts of the blastoderm with enclosed yolk mass. Furthermore only the three first pairs of limbs, the embryonal legs, are formed at the same time, while the following four pairs, the ambulatory legs, are segmented off by degrees from before backward, most frequently one pair after the other and with longer or shorter intervals of time. The ganglia seem to develop contemporaneously with the embryonal limbs, and the ganglia of the abdominal side are divided into two principal sections, a foremost one for the embryonal legs, and a hindmost one for the ambulatory legs; but this latter mass of ganglia is not till a later stage separated into four or five pairs of ganglia by degrees as the ambulatory legs develop. I may refer to my figures pl. I, fig. 11 and pl. II, fig. 18, both representing what I call the second larval stage; the first figure represents *Pseudopallene circularis*, in which the whole mass of ganglia is seen still undivided, and only the nerve mass belonging to the segments of the embryonal legs, has been slightly separated; the other figure represents *Nymphon Sluiteri*, in which the two pairs of ganglionic centra may be distinctly discerned united to a common mass, while the nerve mass of the first pair of ambulatory legs is well separated from the following mass representing the ganglionic mass of the three following pairs of ambulatory legs, in which mass, however, as yet only two pairs of ganglionic centra are to be seen. The larva of *Nymphon Sluiteri* upon the whole is more developed than that of *Pseudopallene*.

Between the embryonal and the larval stage there is no distinct boundary, in so far as this boundary is to be determined by the embryo's leaving the egg; but the embryo leaves the egg sometimes on an earlier, sometimes on a later stage.

I have already before mentioned that according to the common view the limit of the embryonal stage is formed by the embryo breaking the egg shell or egg membrane, and that the whole development taking place before this act, is reckoned to the embryonal stage, but that I cannot agree with this view. As the embryo, however, in the different Pycnogonida, breaks the egg shell sometimes after a shorter, sometimes after a longer development, nay, sometimes not even, until all the limbs, the ambulatory legs included, have been developed, it will be understood that Korschelt and Heider, Lehrb. Entwick. wirbell. Thier. 1890, in their large, well known text book can say of the Pycnogonida that only "die meisten Pantopoden entwickeln sich mittelst Metamorphose", l. c. p. 662, as if there were any important difference between the different Pycnogonida; Dohrn, Pantop. Golf. Neap. 1881, even says l. c. p. 77: "Pallene hat die ganze Larvenentwickelung vollkommen unterdrückt, das junge Thier, welches die Eischale verlässt, besitzt bereits alle definitive Extremitäten, wenn auch noch nicht in definitiver Gestalt". On the following page we find: "Wenn der Embryo seine Reife erreicht hat, gleicht er in vielen Beziehungen der Larve von Phoxichilidium, welche den Hydroidpolypen verlässt". In my opinion the peculiarity in *Pallene emaciata*, the species mentioned by Dohrn, is only to be found in the fact that the larva completes its development in the egg, inside the egg shell; and that this fact is not to be understood as something general in the genus, but only as a peculiarity in this species among known forms I infer from the fact that in another *Pallene*-species, *Pallene hastata*, I have found all larvæ free with only three pairs of developed ambulatory legs, pl. I, fig. 18—19. In the nearly related genus *Pseudopallene* I have even found the larva free in its first stage with the two foremost pairs of ambulatory legs not yet quite developed, pl. I, fig. 8. In the following I shall enter into further details as to this fact. Also in other genera, for inst. in *Nymphon*, it may be found in the different species that the larvæ leave the egg shell sooner or later, without any other difference in the course of development. It is quite another thing that a good boundary really exists, but it can as usual be placed at the origin of the first larval form, here accordingly it is to be applied to the form that has been called "Protonymphon" (Hoek) or the Pantopod-larva (Dohrn).

Already in the introduction to this section on the larval development, I spoke of the usual misconception with regard to the duration of the embryonal life, and gave a quotation from the textbook by Korschelt and Heider. I have here tried by demonstration on my figures to maintain more in detail that all Pycnogonida pass through the same series of larval stages, whether the larva "Protonymphon" frees itself at once, or remains in the egg till all the ambulatory legs are developed, even if it has not attained its full length, segmentation, or all its appendages.

When the yolk-division is equal the whole blastoderm, only excepting the middle and hinder parts of the dorsal side, participates in the formation of the embryonal limbs and the proboscis. The embryo is free at once, is considered to be a fully developed larva in the first stage, and is called Protonymphon (Hoek) or Pantopod-larva kat' exochen (Dohrn, Morgan).

It is the enormous, overruling development of the embryonal limbs and the proboscis that is a characteristic feature of this larval form, and this feature is found spread through the whole system of the Pycnogonida, and has been known and described in different genera, as *Phoxichilidium*, *Pycnogonum*, *Phoxichilus*, *Ammothea (Achelia)*, *Ascorhynchus*, and *Tanystylum*. It is also this larval form which has originally played the greatest part as to the question of the systematic position of the

Pycnogonida in a so-called natural system (phylogenesis), several authors, and especially Dohrn, having thought to find the Nauplius-type in it, a conception that Dohrn, however, as is well known, has again abandoned, comp. his Pantopoden des Golfes von Neapel (1889), the section Phylogenie der Pantopoden, especially p. 87 seq.

When the yolk-division is unequal, only the foremost part of the blastoderm participates in the formation of the embryonal limbs and the proboscis, while the hindmost part of this latter with enclosed macromeres appears as a bag-like dilation behind. The embryo remains wholly or partly in the egg, or, if it leave it, the embryo remains at or on the father.

This larva which is to be regarded as the close of the first larval stage, has hitherto been drawn from a less number of genera than the Protonymphon; besides from the large genus *Nymphon* it is also known from the genera *Pallene*, *Pseudopallene*, and *Zetes* (*Euryeyde*), and I shall also be able to add some new forms. It may, however, sometimes be questioned whether this larval stage here is to be regarded as Protonymphon or not. Thus for instance in the hitherto known species of the genus *Nymphon* a yolk-sack is always found at the close of the first larval stage, but this sack sometimes is so very small, that one may be tempted to regard the larva in this stage as Protonymphon, as has been done by Hoek with regard to *Nymphon gallicum*.

In both forms this larval stage begins with a contemporaneous development of the three pairs of embryonal limbs, i. e. the chelifori and the embryonal legs, each pair of the limbs representing its metamere with the ganglia, and besides an interjacent process with an oral orifice at the point, i. e. the proboscis.

A peculiar position is here occupied by the genera *Pallene* and *Pseudopallene*, which will be bespoken more in detail at the close of this section.

The embryonal limbs accordingly appear at the same time as three pairs of large, flat protuberances, warts, or processes on the under side of the blastoderm, anteriorly enclosing the single protuberance of the proboscis, comp. my figure of the ovum of *Pycnogonum littorale* pl. I, fig. 1. All seven lumps are prolonged in a tubiform manner to lengthy processes, pl. I, fig. 2, the foremost free ends of which in the embryonal limbs are segmented by two consecutive segmentations. Of these three pairs of limbs the foremost pair, the chelifori, are almost from the beginning larger than the others, and grow disproportionately, when compared with those, and the hindmost part, the part arising from the trunk, is also more or less distinctly constricted from this as an independent joint, the scape. Furthermore the fact has also to be mentioned that the two terminal joints of the chelifori always in the larva form a chela or a pair of pincers, so that these limbs get a very great resemblance to the cheke of the Arachnida. It is a matter of course that this congruity with the said organ of the Arachnida must be carefully taken into consideration when the question is of the systematic affinity of the two groups; another question, however, is, how much importance we shall have to attach to it. Finally is here to be mentioned the gland which is most frequently found in the basal part or the scape of the chelifori, and the shorter or longer thorns, arising from this joint.

The two hindmost pairs of limbs, the embryonal legs, are uniform, always much smaller than the chelifori. Their basal part is comparatively short, and never constricted from the body; the first

ment is round and slender, and the second, or outermost, joint is always still thinner, most frequently claw-shaped, and of about the same length as the preceding joint; sometimes, however, this
second joint is prolonged to a long, thin thread more than twice the length of the body, as for inst.
in *Nymphon mixtum comparatum*, pl. I, fig. 4. The growth of the embryonal legs soon ceases, and even if
they, as is often the case, are kept in the following larval stages, they show no alteration.

The proboscis, like the embryonal legs, begins as a low protuberance, soon growing into
a conical process with more or less tapering sides, but without trace of any inner or outer division,
far less of a coalescing of constituent parts. The pharynx, however, is early developed, already in
this larval stage, and it is seen as a dark line stretching from the point of the proboscis towards its
base, as in *Nymphon longitarse*, pl. II, fig. 20, and in *Nymphon macronyx*, pl. II, fig. 9. The chitinous
ridges serving for the insertion of the Musculi retractores of the pharynx, are also early developed.

With regard to the interpretation of the proboscis I shall take the liberty to state my opinion
already in this place, although my interpretation is chiefly due to the structure of this organ found
in a much more advanced stage of development and especially in the imago. It is the unhappy note
by Latreille to his description of the Pycnogonida, Règne animal, éd. II. Tom IV (1829) which is
found again and again. The note, l. c. p. 276, note 3, runs thus: Le siphon . . . m'a offert des sutures
longitudinales, de manière qu'il me paraît composé du labre, de la languette et de deux mâchoires, le
tout soudé ensemble . It was to be thought that Dohrn[1] had succeeded in demolishing this notion,
and I can with all my heart agree with him, when in Pantopoden des Golfes von Neapel (1881) he
says: Wir würden . . . keinenfalls aber an eine Verschmelzung von extremitätenartigen Mundtheilen
zu denken haben , l. c. p. 109. We find nevertheless that Adlerz in his fine little essay, Contributions
to the Morphology of the Pantopoda (Bidrag till Pantopodernes Morfologi (1888)) tries to maintain
the old view of Latreille. Adlerz founds his arguments especially on the fact that the two lowermost antimeres (Dohrn) of the proboscis receive nerves from special centra in the first abdominal
ganglion, comp. his fig. 2 on pl. I, and the letters *a* and *ug* in this figure. For these two foremost
centra with their fibrillous punctuous mass (Leydig: Punktmasse) in connection with the two
pairs of centra behind them in the same ganglion should show, how this ganglion is composed of
three original pairs of ganglia, but it is well known that to each pair of ganglia belongs a metamere
with a pair of limbs, which metamere could not then be anything but the two lowermost antimeres
l. c. p. 10. To this is to be answered that, as no trace of limbs has ever been seen that might correspond to or be merged in the two antimeres, as little has any trace been found of a pair of foremost,
free ganglia; besides it has to be remembered that the supply of nerves for the two lowermost metameres most properly must be said to arise from the foremost one of the two, originally separated,
but now coalesced pairs of ganglia, in which, but not until a later stage, the corresponding foremost
pair of centra have developed. This view would also agree with my examinations, as I have also
found the ganglia to be originally uniform, and not until later showing distinct centra with their
fibrillous punctuous mass running into or stretching into the nerves of the limbs. I think upon
the whole that as to the morphology too great stress is at present laid upon the ganglia, and my

[1] Already Zenker in Untersuchungen über die Pycnogoniden (1852) has p. 383 seq. rejected the supposition of
Latreille referring to the representation given by Kröyer of the occurrence of the proboscis in the young larva.

examinations of the development of the Pycnogonida seem to me to show that in these animals the separation of the nerve mass into ganglia only takes place by degrees, contemporaneously with a corresponding separation of the somites of the trunk, and the separation and growth of the limbs, comp. my figures of the first larval stages in *Nymphon macronyx*, pl. II, fig. 9, *Pseudopallene circularis*, pl. I, fig. 11, and *Nymphon Sluiteri*, pl. II, fig. 18, and with these figures may be compared the abdominal nerve cord in *Pseudopallene circularis* in the second and ¦third larval stage, pl. I, fig. 12 and 15. Upon the whole I doubt very much that a coalescing of well separated limbs really takes place, and so much I know at all events from my own examinations that the union, supposed to take place of the arms of the second pair of feet in the females of Lernæopoda to a fastening knob, is only apparent, each arm in reality ending in an independent knob; the two knobs are only more or less loosely joined to a single knob — by a somewhat strong pressure they are easily separated. As a paradigm on the coalescing of limbs this pair at all events cannot be used.

The proboscis is thus, after its origin and structure, especially the want of limbs, not homologous with the other metameres of the body; but even if it be something particular, or, to use the expression of Dohrn organum sui generis, it can in no way be said of it, as does this author, that im ganzen bisherigen Arthropodentypus nicht seines Gleichen, nicht einmal etwas ihm Aehnliches is found, Pantop. Golf. Neap. 1881, p. 13, for I suppose that the proboscis of the Pycnogonida will be found throughout the class of Arachnida, the only difference being that here it is free, large, and predominant, while in the other Arachnida it most frequently is very small and hidden between the gnathites. As an instance of a free proboscis in the Arachnida I shall refer to what in the following is said of the genus *Koenenia*. As I have already indicated in the foregoing, in the chapter on the terminology, p. 3, there is still less reason to interpret it as, or give it the name of, head. A similar structure of the mouth is otherwise found in some mites, as it also in several respects reminds of the mouth in some higher, sucking worms (*Hirudo*). In the Insecta, especially in the Tipulida, we find a parallel in the structure of the gullet; and as well in the Pycnogonida as in the Tipulida the production of a pumping or sucking apparatus may be thought to be the conditional reason of the common plan of structure. I think it may be taken to be a consequence of simple, mechanical laws that, when a tube with firm walls is to form a pumping or sucking apparatus, the easiest thing will be to place three plates with contiguous margins longitudinally in the the tube, and by ropes or other suitable means make those plates to approach the wall of the tube at the same time, by which motion the inner opening will be increased, and a pumping or sucking be brought about. With regard to the Tipulæ I may refer to my paper, The Gnathites of the Flies. Trophi Dipterorum (1881). On pl. II, fig. 10 of this paper is found a transverse section of the gullet of a Tipulid of the triangular form, so well known from a number of figures and transverse sections of the proboscis of the Pycnogonida.

For the elucidation of the morphological significance of the proboscis I may also refer to the figures in a recent work by two Danish zoologists, the doctors H. J. Hansen and Will. Sorensen: The Order Palpigradi Thor. (Koenenia mirabilis Grassi) and its Relationship to the other Arachnida (1898). This Arachnid has already earlier been the subject of a detailed examination and a systematical view by Grassi: I Progenitori dei Miriapodi e degli Insetti. Memoria V. Intorno ad un nuovo

3

Archetile attrogastro (Koenenia mirabilis) rappresentante di un nuovo ordine (Microtelyphonida) esso, which essay follows the preliminary paper without figures by the same author: Intorno ad un nuovo Aracnide attrogastro (Koenenia mirabilis) che crediamo rappresentante d'un nuovo ordine Microteliphonida (1885). As, however, the treatment by Hansen and Sorensen seems to me to be far more solid than that of Grassi, and as the figures, in which I take most interest, are very fine and distinct, I shall chiefly abide by this treatise written in English, with its plate, to the figure 2 of which I shall especially refer, as it shows the animal viewed from the lower side. The homology of the proboscis of *Koenenia* (or, which by the authors have been named with the unfortunate expression mouth, while Grassi uses the much better one papilla boccale, with the proboscis of the Protonymphon is conspicuous, and the relation and situation as to the three foremost pairs of limbs is exactly the same. Through the proboscis of *Koenenia* a transition is next formed to the mouth-structure in the other Arachnida, where I, contrary to Hansen and Sorensen, and to the prevalent opinion, find the same proboscis, and it has only to be pointed out that the proboscis in the other orders of Arachnida, on account of its position between the powerful gnathites, necessarily must become shorter and more strongly chitinous than in *Koenenia*; and nowhere, perhaps, is the shortening and chitinization so accomplished as in the Telyphona[1] so nearly related to *Koenenia*. But if the proboscis of *Koenenia* and thus of the other Arachnida is homologous with that of the Pycnogonida, and if it has never been supposed or is impossible to consider the proboscis of *Koenenia* as formed by a coalescing of oral parts or gnathites, then it must be said that there is no reason at all to suppose such a coalescing in the proboscis of the Pycnogonida.

In the figures 7 and 8 is next given a drawing of the proboscis of *Koenenia*, viewed from the side and from below, but without any contribution as to its inner structure; it is only said that the muscles are very strong, and some fine, indistinct lines in fig. 7 may be taken as an indication of these muscles. It cannot, however, be doubted that it is a sucking apparatus or a pump, as is also shown even by a less strict examination.

The genera *Pallene* and *Pseudopallene* show in their larval form, as well in the first as in the second stage, so great a difference when compared with the other larvæ of Pycnogonida, that there might seem to be reason enough to set them up as a particular type; but as the difference chiefly consists of a reduction of the embryonal legs or even a disappearing of these, it is morphologically of small importance. I have not seen so young a stage as that I have drawn of *Pycnogonum littorale* pl. 1, fig. 1 and 2; the youngest stage I have seen, is that of *Pseudop. spinipes*, pl. 1, fig. 7, where the embryo is viewed from the side, lying in the egg, and with distinctly defined cheliforus, proboscis, and foremost pair of ambulatory legs. In the cheliforus, the two outermost joints, the chela, are not yet separated, and every trace of embryonal legs is wanting. That the swelling behind the cheliforus must be the foremost pair of ambulatory legs, and cannot be one of the two pairs of embryonal legs,

---

[1] Thus I cannot agree to the comparison between the proboscis mouth of *Koenenia* and the composite mouth, with regard to addition of the gnathites of the other Arthropoda, and I think that the difference as to the mouth-structure may best be expressed in this manner that, while in the Arthropoda generally more pairs of limbs, the gnathites, close around the oral door or orifice, and are developed with reference to their partaking in the catching of and preliminary treatment with the food, in *Koenenia*, as well as in the Pycnogonida, all the corresponding limbs are kept away from the oral door and accordingly in these forms is placed freely in the point of the papilla boccale.

is shown by the series of larval forms, given in the following figures 8-11, and 16-17 of *Pseudo-pallene spinipes* and *circularis*, as well as of *Pallene brevirostris*; as they, however, belong to the second larval stage, they will be mentioned more in detail in a following section. It may be possible, of course, that I can have overlooked rudimentary larval legs; but in a somewhat later stage of the same species I have seen no trace of these legs either, and as, in all places where I have observed them, they have only appeared as one or two pairs of short, inarticulate processes, I am inclined to suppose that here they have been quite absent. Of still less importance is the peculiarity that the foremost pair of ambulatory legs have begun to appear so early, before the chelifori were quite developed, and before the byssus-gland was formed. The two genera mentioned here must be supposed to pass a great part of the second larval stage in the egg-shell.

Morgan, Contrib. Embryol. 1891 has not in *Pallene empusa* seen any trace of the foremost pair of the embryonal legs, though he has seen some trace of the second pair; at all events I understand the following quotation in that way, l. c. p. 14. On the sides of the body, just in front of the first pair of ambulatory legs, are a pair of projections, one on each side. These are the beginning of the third pair of limbs — the ovigerous legs. I have seen no traces of the second pair of appendages in the ontogeny of Pallene .

In the basal part of the chelifori is most frequently found a large gland, the byssus-gland, with an excretory duct opening through a shorter or longer hollow thorn in the fore-margin of the said basal part.

The occurrence of a large gland in the chelifori has already been mentioned by Dohrn and Hoek, who have also given descriptions and figures of it; by Morgan it is only drawn in the chelifori of *Tanystylum orbiculatum*; cp. the following.

This gland, the byssus gland, is most frequently distinctly conspicuous, and through the epidermis it is seen to consist of a circle of large glandular cells gathered round a hollow, or reservoir, from which an excretory duct is seen to lead to the inner fore-end of the basal part of the cheliforus, comp. the enlarged figure of the fore-end of the larva of *Nymphon grossipes*, pl. I, fig. 22. In *Nymphon elegans*, pl. II, fig. 16, I have found the gland to be almost as distinct and of the same structure; while it was far less distinct in *Nymphon longitarse*, pl. II, fig. 19-20, *Nymphon robustum*, pl. II, fig. 6, *Nymphon macronyx*, pl. II, fig. 11, and in *Nymphon spinosum*, pl. II, fig. 13; but possibly it was not quite developed, and so was not so well preserved in the spirit. The excretory duct opens into the basal end of a shorter or longer hollow thorn, through the point of which the gland-secretion is produced as a very thin thread of a considerable length. The thread, which stains strongly (I have in all instances used picro-carmine), is easily seen, and is also to be seen in my figures of the larvæ. The development of the gland begins very early in the embryonic stage on the border of the basal end of the cheliforus and the corresponding metamere, but it is not finished until later in the first larval stage, when the larva has left the egg wholly, or, at all events, with the fore part. The length of the excretory thorn varies very much; generally it is short or even very short, but it can, as in *Pycnogonum littorale*, gain a very considerable length, about the length of the embryonal legs, cp. pl. I, fig. 3, where, however, the limit between the thorn and the free thread, which limit is difficult to see, has not been indicated. The genera, in which I have found a distinct gland with a thread arising t an t, as Nymph n, Phoxi nium, Pseudopallene, and Pallene. In the last-mentioned genus, however, I have in Pa brevirostris found, in stead of a single thread originating from the common gland, a bundle of seven, rather short, somewhat curled threads each issuing from an excretory duct of its own, pl. I, fig. 16 and 17. I have seen no gland from which any of these threads might arise; but I think it also probable, in comparison with what Hoek has found in Nymphon hamatum, what I shall presently recur to, that each of the seven threads arises from a cell of its own. In Phoxichilidium co. rutum I have found no trace of these glands, nor of their thorns and threads; the threads drawn on pl I, fig. 4, are the outermost joints of the embryonal legs, which are prolonged in a bristlelike manner, and probably replace the wanting byssus-threads; this larva, with its parasitic way of living, has no use for the hooks, to which in the other Pycnogonida the outermost joint of the embryonal legs has been transformed. In Paranymphon spinosum¹, pl. II, fig. 22 24, I have found indistinct traces of the gland and excretory duct, and the thorns were long and closed. In Zetes hispidus, pl. II, fig. 27, I have found a distinct gland, but no excretory duct from it, and also here the thorns were closed. It may be possible that in the two last-mentioned cases a reduction of a commonly occurring organ has taken place, as it would seem to be natural in Phoxichilidium; but it may also be supposed that we have here a stage of transition from a simpler organ to the more perfect byssus-gland.

Dohrn and Hoek have already earlier described and drawn this gland, and Dohrn especially, in Bau u. Entwick. Arthrop. 1870, has from the larva in the first stage of Achelia lævis (= Ammothea lævis) Taf. V, fig. 7, given a figure of the gland with its excretory duct and a secretion-thread (byssus) projecting from the long, pointed, hollow thorn, but from Pycnogonum littorale in a similar stage only the hollow thorn, he, as it would appear, not having seen the thread, not to speak of the gland. In the text he, when speaking of Achelia lævis, describes the gland rather copiously, but says nothing of its use or importance, l. c. p. 141 seq. Hoek, in Report Pycnog. Challenger, 1881, draws this gland in Nymphon brevicollum and N. longicoxa, pl. XX, fig. 2 and 5, and names it in the explanation to the plates Spinning apparatus in the mandible. In another Nymphon, N. hamatum, pl. XX, fig. 3 and 4 he draws, instead of the common gland, a whole heap of single miliary gland cells each cell with its own secretion-thread. No doubt this last form of glands with its threads corresponds to the bundles of threads I have mentioned in Pallene brevirostris; and as in the last-mentioned species the gland was different in structure from that of the other species of the same or of nearly related genera, so is also the structure of the gland in Nymphon hamatum peculiar, compared with that in all the many species of Nymphon, from which the gland is known. Hoek in his text, l. c. p. 141, compares the secretion-threads to the byssus-threads of the Lamellibranchiata, which comparison I have found so appropriate that I have given to the gland itself the name of byssus-gland. Dohrn generally draws the byssus-gland of the larvæ of which he gives figures, but he does not always indicate it by special letters; when he does so, he gives the letters HD, which in the explanation to the plates are rendered as Hautdrüsen, and DHD, which are rendered as Ausführungs-gang der Hautdrüsen. In the text they are mentioned in the section entitled, Geschlechtsorgane und Entwickelung, especially on p. 70 seq., and here Barana arenicola is also pronounced destitute

¹ See table on pl. II

of the excretory duct and thorn in contradistinction to *Barana Castelli*. Hoek, in Nouv. étud. Pycnog., 1881, draws the gland with excretory duct and thorn in *Ammothea longipes*, pl. XXX, fig. 40, and in *Pycnogonum littorale*, pl. XXX, fig. 45, as well as the gland alone in *Nymphon gallicum*, pl. XXX, fig. 43.

The descriptions and figures of Dohrn, as well as most of those of Hoek do not very much resemble those given by me; but I suppose that they generally represent a younger stage in the development of the gland, whereas my figures, especially of the larva of *Nymphon grossipes*, pl. I, fig. 22, and those by Hoek of *Nymphon longicoxa*, Report Pycnog. Challenger, pl. XX, fig. 5, which figures are very much alike, show the fully developed stage.

Morgan, in Contrib. Embryol., 1891, has drawn the byssus-gland in the larva of *Tanystylum orbiculatum*, pl. IV, fig. IX, in a shape most resembling my figure of the gland in *Nymphon grossipes*. Else Morgan does not mention the gland at all.

I have been rather long in speaking of this gland, partly because it seems to me to have hitherto been somewhat overlooked, and partly because I suppose it to have some morphological, systematic importance, compared with the poison-gland in the corresponding pair of limbs in the Arachnida. Possibly it might also be compared with the gland which Dohrn has described by the name of secretory organ, and which he mentions as occurring in the palps and the ovigerous legs, or, where these limbs are wanting, in the corresponding metameres. I think at all events this comparison to be more obvious than the comparison with the sexual glands; comp. Dohrn, Pantop. Golf. Neap. 1881, his Excretionsorgane and the following paragraph, Geschlechtsorgane und Entwickelung, p. 63 seq.

The development of the second larval stage begins with the growing of the hindmost segment of the trunk, and the separation of a foremost ring with the first pair of hind limbs, or ambulatory legs, upon which in a similar way the second and third pairs of ambulatory legs are separated, while the fourth pair and the caudal segment are seen behind as a three-cleft appendage. At the close of the development of this stage the embryonal legs have fallen off, but the imaginal limbs and forelimbs, the palps and ovigerous legs, have not appeared, if they appear at all. Only very rarely the chelifori fall off already on this stage. The byssus-gland is kept till the development of the stage is finished.

The development of the second stage does not take place at once, but through more or fewer castings of the skin, and in such a way, that sometimes a greater, sometimes a smaller interval is found between the origin and the development of each of these three pairs of ambulatory legs, while, however, the consecutive order is kept. Perhaps it may be called a little arbitrary to limit the second stage in the way we have done here, as in some species so great a pause may occur during the stage, especially after the development of the second pair of ambulatory legs, as is the case in *Pseudopallene circularis*, that we might as well place the limit of a larval stage after the development of the second pair as after that of the third pair; in most Pycnogonid-larvæ, however, the development is evenly advancing, till the third pair of ambulatory legs have been developed.

As in the preceding section the genera *Pallene* and *Pseudopallene* were especially mentioned on account of their peculiarity, so we shall also here mention these genera as the last, and for the same reason likewise delay the examination of the genus *Phoxichilidium*.

The genus *Nymphon*, which is, together with the subgenera *Boreonymphon* and *Chætonymphon*, chiefly a palearctic form, presents by its numerous species and great extension the best opportunity for European naturalists in these northern countries to make a continuous study of the development of the Pycnogonid larvæ. It is also *Nymphon grossipes* of which we have the most detailed representation, already given by Kröyer, Kmdsk. Pycnog. (1845), as it is also this species I shall use, and, with reference to my figures, pl. I, fig. 21–25, give a representation of its development during this stage.

On the preceding figure, pl. I, fig. 20, representing the beginning of the second stage, is seen, besides the three pairs of embryonal limbs, also the beginning of the two foremost pairs of ambulatory legs, though only slightly pronounced; but in fig. 21, which absolutely belongs to the second stage, the first pair of ambulatory legs are already much developed, of about the same length as the trunk, and with the last joint well developed to a bent, strong claw with two slender thorns, the auxiliary claws, arising from the dorsal side near the base; the articulation of the leg, however, have not proceeded farther than to five joints exclusive of the claw. The second pair of ambulatory legs have not been developed farther than to form a cylindrical process without any articulation or claw, neither are in the body itself the corresponding segments conspicuous, which latter circumstance, perhaps, may be due to a not quite good preservation. The byssus-gland, however, is now fully developed, and the byssus-thread is distinctly seen to originate from the middle of the gland. In the following figure, fig. 22, the fore-end of the larva has been represented much more enlarged to show distinctly the structure of the byssus-gland. In the same figure the yolk-mass in the foremost part of the body is also seen to consist of small particles (the micromeres?) smaller than those of the hindmost part (the macromeres?), of which, however, only a small portion has been represented; a particular interspace between the two yolk-masses is also distinctly seen. In fig. 23 the larva is represented much more developed, but still in the second stage; both the foremost pairs of ambulatory legs are now well developed, all nine joints, inclusive of the claw, being well separated, and the two auxiliary claws very large; the third pair of legs are also rather long, four-jointed, but the last joint not yet claw-shaped, and there is no indication of any auxiliary claws; the fourth pair of legs and the hindmost part of the trunk form a solid body, while short curves behind indicate the wanting pairs of limbs; anteriorly in the trunk the transverse-oval eye-knob with indistinct eyes is seen; the byssus-threads are still present. Fig. 24 shows the same larva from the lower side, and it shows how the yolk mass not only fills the whole trunk, but also sends long processes into the three pairs of ambulatory legs. The yolk is surrounded by a distinct sheath, seen with special distinctness in the third pair of legs, and forming the walls of the intestine canal during the following development. Before, on both sides of the proboscis, the embryonal legs are still seen, but they are now decaying, the matrix, or pulp — as it was called in the old times — shrinking, and being consumed (?). In fig. 25 the embryonal legs have been represented still more enlarged, by which means also the epidermis of the legs is distinctly seen in contradistinction to the pulp, and where it is seen to have preserved its former size and firmness, only the point of the outermost joint being a little retracted; an even shrinking or resorption of the embryonal legs, or, at all events, of their exoskeleton is accordingly out of the question, we must suppose them to be thrown off at once.

In his first essay, ‹Om Pycnogonidernes Forvandling› (On the metamorphosis of the Pycnogonida) 1849, Kroyer already gives a rather detailed description of this stage, but of the embryonal legs he has only seen one pair; his words are (l. c. p. 303): ‹Between the chelifori and the first pair of feet I have sometimes seen projecting on the side a little process, fig. 3 c, appearing to consist of only two joints and of a length of abt. $\frac{1}{48}$''' (Danish); after its position I think it must be taken to be the first trace of the palps. The interpretation by Kroyer of this little organ, to be sure, was not correct; but to this question I shall recur in the following, in the section on the *Pseudopallene*-larva; here I shall only add that the figure of the larva itself, fig. 3 a, is bad, and consequently the reproduction of this figure and other ones from his plate III, as they are given after the drawings by Thornam, in the work of travel of Gaimard (1849) pl. 39, fig. 1 a —g, must be considered as a great progress. In the work of travel the new principal figure, fig. 1 d, resembles very well our fig. 23, and the pointed thorns or hooks with which also the limbs behind the chelifori here are seen to end, agree very well with the outermost joint or hook of the embryonal legs, but not with the imaginal fore limbs in any stage whatever.

The second species the development of which I have been able to follow, is *Nymphon robustum*, and I shall here describe the second stage, referring to my figures, pl. II, fig. 2—6. A peculiarity of this species, when compared with most of the other species, is the long time, during which the larva remains confined in the egg-shell, or the egg-membrane and cast-off larval sloughs[1]. The first stage of the larva in my possession is the second stage, shown in fig. 2: here the larva is seen enclosed behind by two membranes besides the egg-shell, and that it is not only the trunk which has cast off its slough, may be seen from the proboscis, of which one cast-off slough is seen enclosed in the other, as I have shown it more distinctly by a special figure, fig. 3. In fig. 2 otherwise, all four pairs of ambulatory legs are seen in a course of development, the first pair as usual farther proceeded than the others, but still only with slight constrictions indicating the beginning articulation. The segmentation of the trunk is already here discernible, and it may also be observed that the first pair of embryonal legs more than usually are distinguished by being earlier developed and thicker than the second pair; as it is the case with the first pair of ambulatory legs, the old slough is also here seen loosely wrapping the first pair of embryonal legs. In fig. 4 showing a stage a little more advanced, the proboscis as well as the abdomen is seen lying in the two last sloughs; the second pair of ambulatory legs have here grown comparatively more than any of the other limbs; besides the byssus-threads are now secerned. In fig. 5 and 6 the development has proceeded still farther, the two foremost pairs of ambulatory legs are completely articulated, while the third pair is still much shorter than the others, and the articulation not quite finished. In fig. 6 showing the larva from the lower side, the byssus-gland is developed. The auxiliary claws are as a rule very small though quite distinct, which feature is characteristic of the species.

Of *Nymphon macronyx* I possess, besides the larva on the first stage mentioned in the fore-

[1] It is also this species that for a longer time than any other Pycnogonid clings to the ovigerous legs of the father; comp. the representation of this fact by Hoek, Pycnog. Willem Barents, 1881, Taf. II, fig. 35.

... ng, also a couple of larvæ on the second stage, but not of the same degree of development. In the younger of these larvæ, pl. II, fig. 11, the three foremost pairs of ambulatory legs are all developed, and, contrary to what commonly is the case, all developed to the same degree. The byssus-gland is also earlier developed than usual. In the somewhat older larva, fig. 12, the first pair of ambulatory legs are, as usual, much more developed than the second pair, and the third pair is not even to be seen.

Of *Nymphon Sluiteri* I have also drawn a phase of the second stage, pl. II, fig. 17, viewed from the side, and fig. 18, viewed from below, but they show nothing remarkable with regard to the development of the limbs.

Of *Pycnogonum littorale* I have an interesting drawing, pl. I, fig. 4. The specimen was taken a score of years ago by the present doctores, Mr. Hector Jungersen and Mr. Johannes Petersen, at Frederikshavn without particular statements as to the circumstances in which it was found. It can be no other than a larva in the close of the second stage of a *Pycnogonum* s. str., but from Frederikshavn and upon the whole from Denmark we know of no other *Pycnogonum* than *P. littorale*, which moreover is commonly found on the locality in question. The embryonal limbs have already quite disappeared, and no traces are to be seen, either from the upper side, represented here, or from the lower side. That these limbs have disappeared is no wonder, as they usually do so, if not so quickly, at all events in a short time; more remarkable is the absence of the chelifori. In other instances the chelifori are embryonal limbs which are kept throughout the life of the animal, if not always with a fully developed chela, at all events, though, with fragments of it, and only in a few forms, the genera *Pycnogonum* and *Phoxichilus*, the so-called order *Accrata* of Sars, and in his family *Colossendeidæ*, the chelifori are quite wanting in the full-grown animal; there is, however, a great possibility that the chelifori of the last-mentioned family are not thrown off until an advanced stage, after the close of the larval development. Such, at all events, is the case in *Colossendeis angusta* (and *gracilis*) according to the observations of Hoek, which observations I shall here augment very much (in another *Coloss.* (*macerrima*) I have found the chelifori thrown off already in a very young animal. The larva of *Pycnogonum* drawn here, is, judging by the development of the ambulatory legs, in the close of the second stage, all three pairs of legs having reached the full segmentation, also the claw. The body and the legs are smooth and naked, without the thick, rugged exoskeleton distinguishing the grown *Pycnogonum*, and only the oculiferous tubercle and the three knobs in the middle line of the back remind of the rugged appearance of the animal. The first segment of the trunk is uncommonly and unproportionally large.

The genera *Pallene* and *Pseudopallene* are distinguished from the other Pycnogonida, not only by the above mentioned absence, or rudimentary state of the embryonal legs, but also by the two foremost pairs of ambulatory legs arising contemporaneously, growing, and attaining to a considerable development, before the growth of the third pair of legs begins. Of *Pallene* I have examined two species, *Pall. brevirostris* and *Pall. hastata*. The former, *Pall. brevirostris*, is given on a rather early stage, in which the two pairs of ambulatory legs are somewhat short and thick, with a single construction in the middle besides the claw, pl. I, fig. 16; a special distinction is the separation, already mentioned in the foregoing, of the byssus-gland in particular dermal glands, each with a byssus-thread

of its own, seven glands on each side of the animal, fig. 17 a. a. Of *Pall. hastata* I have two figures, pl. I,
fig. 18—19, which show a more advanced stage, the third pair of ambulatory legs being here already
very much lengthened, so that all three pairs seem to have been developed at the same time; from
the first figure, however, it is distinctly seen, that there must have been an interval between the
second and third pair. In the species of *Pseudopallene* the delay of the third pair of ambulatory legs,
is, however, much more considerable, as is already shown by the two figures of *Pseudop. spinipes*,
pl. I, fig. 8 9. As to the further development I shall refer to the figures of *Pseudop. circularis*, pl. I,
fig. 10- 14. In the two first of these figures the development has not gone farther than to the representation of *Pseudop. spinipes*, given in the preceding figure, but in fig. 12 it has gone much farther.
Here the two foremost pairs of ambulatory legs have been fully developed (of the four uniform legs
only the foremost right leg has been drawn), while the leg of the third pair is still only a bag-shaped
process with a characteristic stiff bristle implanted on the upper side, a little before the point. In the
same figure is furthermore seen the processes of the intestinal canal into the three pairs of legs,
going in the wholly drawn foremost leg quite into the outermost joint. No traces of embryonal legs
are seen, but neither, what is to be emphasized, is the least beginning of the imaginal fore limbs to
be found. In the fore edge of the first abdominal ganglion, or the suboesophageal ganglion are seen
through the epidermis a pair of short processes, as also a pair of still smaller, ballshaped appendages
farther back, inside the side margin; but no nervous fibres are seen to arise from these processes and
appendages. The anus is now distinctly open. Fig. 13 represents the same larva from the upper side,
but with the two foremost pairs of ambulatory legs completely removed; the oculiferous tubercle with
the eyes is distinctly seen. Fig. 14 gives the last phase of the same stage. Here also the third pair
of ambulatory legs have been almost fully developed, only the last joint but one wanting; but still
the lower side of the first segment of the trunk is as naked as in the preceding phase, fig. 12.

Kroyer, in his second essay, Bidr. til Kundsk. om Pycnog. (1844), has given a description of
what he calls the first and second stages of *Pallene intermedia* (= *Pseudopallene circularis*); but the
description itself, and still more the figures in Gaimard's work of travel (1849) pl. 39, fig. 2 a. a.— d., of
which figures Kroyer, no doubt, has been thinking, show distinctly that we here have two phases
of the same larval stage, i. e. of the second stage, of which Kroyer treats, and the figures given by
Kroyer of the animals, fig. 2, *a.* and *c.* are completely answering to my figures 8 and 12 -13, only
that in the first of my figures I have also the byssus-thread, and in the last one also the eyes. The
omission of the eyes may, I think, be due to the bad preservation of the larva whereby the elements
of sight have been removed from their position on the oculiferous tubercle; at least I believe to have
found these elements strewn round in the trunk of the original piece of Kroyer which I have had
occasion for examining, as well as the fresh specimen drawn here. Otherwise I think it to be the
real or apparent want of genuine embryonal legs, and the contemporaneous development of the two
foremost pairs of ambulatory legs, by which these latter get a certain resemblance to the former limbs,
which has induced Kroyer not only to suppose this degree of the second larval stage to be the
first, but also, what is much worse, led him to the wrong supposition of the real embryonal legs
developing into the two foremost pairs of ambulatory legs. But this same mistake, on the other
hand, has freed Kroyer from the present common wrong interpretation of the imaginal fore limbs

4'

as first continuations of the embryonal legs. For my part I must regard it as a decided fact that in all Pycnogonida the embryonal legs are quite thrown off during the second larval stage, and that they are in no way identical with the later imaginal fore limbs, the palps and the ovigerous legs, which latter also, and of this there is no doubt, arise, although on the same metameres, still in other parts of these metameres. The two genera mentioned here, *Pallene* and *Pseudopallene*, also show that even if greater or smaller rudiments of the embryonal legs are found in the first larval stage, these rudiments have quite disappeared in the second stage, so that here no trace of limbs is found, from which a new development might arise.

The second larval stage of *Phoxichilidium* shows, in accordance with the parasitical habits of the animal, a quite particular development. I have myself only had the first stage for examination; but as this larva has repeatedly been the object of thorough examinations, I may nevertheless, relying on these examinations, give a short survey of the development of its second stage, founded on the representation by G. Adlerz, Bidrag till Pantop. Morphol. 1888, especially referring to his figures 1—12 in the two accompanying plates. The second larval stage then begins with the disappearing of both pairs of embryonal legs, so that only slight traces or remnants are left. After a couple of moultings, during which the rudimentary remnants of the legs by and by quite disappear, the imaginal limbs are begun, in the common way and in the common order, without, however, breaking through the outer, common, wrapping membrane, until all the traces of the embryonal legs have disappeared. Adlerz now supposes the foremost pair of imaginal fore limbs (II) i. e. the palps, to be begun, cp. his fig. 10, upon which follows the further development of this pair of limbs in fig. 11 and fig. 4 (pl. I); but in the first place the genus *Phoxichilidium* as imago has upon the whole no palps (only the ovigerous legs are found in the male), and next both pairs of fore limbs arise from the lower side of the animal in the way common in Arthropoda, by the growth of a little cellular mass, while Adlerz makes the extremity II develop as the other limbs of the Pycnogonida, especially the ambulatory legs, by a swelling of the sides of the blastoderm or the ectoderm. According to this I cannot take the small tubercles (II) on the side of the trunk to be the future ovigerous legs. Neither can I have any great confidence in the representation or interpretation by Adlerz of the ganglionic string in *Phoxichilidium*, cp. his fig. 4, pl. I; at all events, it does not agree well with his figure of the same string in *Nymphon Strœmii*, which latter figure I take to be correct. In my opinion the ganglion ng which he interprets as undre svælggangliet (the nether pharyngeal ganglion), and from which a nerve is seen to branch off to the extremity II (it ought to be extr. III, as the former extremity is wanting in all Phoxichilidia), must be the ganglion from the first segment of the trunk plus the coalesced ganglia from the metameres of the embryonal legs, or, as it might also be called, the nethermost pharyngeal ganglion. Accordingly I think that after the description of this larva by Adlerz is neither here to be found any continuity between the second pair of embryonal legs and the ovigerous legs of the male.

Semper, Pycnog. und Larvent. 1874, who, like Adlerz, takes it to be the second extremity (=, i. e. the palps, which grows to a little protuberance (beyond which, for the rest, it never passes) seek to remove the difficulties by identifying the first pair of ambulatory legs with the completely disappeared second pair of embryonal legs, which is then marked as 3 I in his figures, pl. 16 and 17, fig. 3—12. If Semper had known the development of more Pycnogonid-larvæ, his explanation would immediately have appeared impossible to himself.

Morgan, Contrib. Embryol. 1891, has found in *Pallene empusa*, p. 24 seq. the same development as I have found in my two species of that genus. I dare not, however, say of the development of the three foremost pairs of ambulatory legs that it is simultaneously, even if the interval between the second and third pair is only small, as has been already observed. Nor can I, as is seen by the foregoing, agree with Morgan as to the fact that this third pair (i. e. the rudimentary embryonal legs) grow out again to form the ovigerous legs. Finally I do not find that *Pallene* with *Pseudo-pallene* deviates so much from the ordinary Pycnogonid-development, that there is sufficient reason to finish, as does Morgan, the description of its ontogeny in the following way: The development of Pallene has become so much abbreviated that there is only a trace of the true Pantopod-larva found in its ontogeny, cp. the foregoing.

Dohrn, Bau u. Entwickl. Arthrop., 1870, p. 144—51, gives a detailed description of *Achelia* (*Ammothea*) *lævis*, and in pl. VI, fig. 11—13 he draws three consecutive stages of the development of this animal, of which three stages I refer his first (in the explanation of the plates called mittleres Stadium) and second stages to my second stage. In the corresponding figures, fig. 11 and 12, the embryonal legs are still seen fully developed, with the exception that the last pair in fig. 12 are somewhat smaller than the other embryonal legs; but judging by my examinations, I regard the smaller size, cp. also my fig. 24 on pl. I, as a consequence of the fact that only the empty sheaths are left, and that besides the points or outermost joints of these sheaths, as in my figure, are retracted, partly into the preceding joint; I cannot suppose a reduction or real diminution of this pair of legs to have taken place. Also the larvæ given by Dohrn, Pantop. Golf. Neap. 1881, pl. XI, fig. 21 and 24, and determined as *Phoxichilus vulgaris*, must be referred to our second larval stage; but the specific determination, especially with regard to the last figure, seems to me to be very doubtful. The first figure, fig. 21, represents a normal Pycnogonid-development, in which I only think it to be not very probable that a *Phoxichilus* should have kept its chelifori so long, and not rather have lost them, either by reduction or throwing off, while the nearly related *Pycnogonum* has wholly lost them before the close of the stage, cp. my figure, pl. I, fig. 4. The improbability that *Phoxichilus* should have kept the chelifori so long, is of course greater with regard to the older larva, fig. 24, *Pycnogonum* having lost them on a little earlier stage. But I am still more unable to believe that the imaginal fore limbs, of which only the hindmost pair are developed and kept only in the male, should commence and begin a development which was soon to be stopped or reduced; for I think it a fact that admits of no doubt, that the appendages, marked in fig. 24 with II and III, are not rudimentary, reduced remnants of the embryonal legs, but on the contrary a beginning development of the imaginal fore limbs.

The third larval stage begins, when the fourth pair of ambulatory legs, which have until now been far behind in development, together with the interjacent caudal segment, begin to grow and develop, until they obtain their permanent shape, the legs resembling the three foregoing pairs. The imaginal fore limbs, palps, and ovigerous legs now appear, after the embryonal legs and sometimes the chelifori have been thrown off, the byssus-gland reduced, and the byssus-threads disappeared. Moultings also take place during the development of this larval stage, until the animal as a young one obtains its complete shape, and now only grows in size and outer investment of thorns and bristles; not till now appear the genital pores, or openings, and the gland-pores.

The point of the development of this stage which is of most interest, is the rise and growth or development of the imaginal fore limbs. Of the two pairs of limbs the foremost one, the palps, seem to develop a little earlier and somewhat faster than the hindmost one, the ovigerous legs, but I have too few examinations to venture to regard it as a rule or law. Where one or both pairs are wanting in the grown animal, probably neither of them appear at all.

I have drawn the third larval stage of *Nymphon grossipes*, pl. I, fig. 26—29, *N. robustum*, pl. II, fig. 7, *N. spinosum*, pl. II, fig. 14, and *Pseudopallene circularis*, pl. I, fig. 15. Besides the general remarks stated above, I must especially point out that the palps immediately at their appearance are found in quite another place than the first pair of embryonal legs just disappeared, that is to say, quite anteriorly behind the base of the proboscis, at a considerable distance from the ovigerous legs, while both pairs of embryonal legs from their rise to their being thrown off are almost in contact at their base, arising together from the hindmost part of the lower surface of the first chief division, cp. fig. 27 *a* and *b* with fig. 24 *b* and *c*.   Furthermore the palps in the first species are sure enough proportionally considerably longer than the ovigerous legs, but in the palps the segmentation is at most only indicated, a fact intimating that no moulting has taken place after the beginning of the limbs, and that these latter have only arisen during this phase of the third stage. In the fourth species, *Pseudop. circularis*, of course only the ovigerous legs have arisen, but their development has not gone farther than to their being segmented inside the smooth epidermis, and thus they have not reached the second phase. The small particular drawings that in pl. I, fig. 28 and 29 have been given of the first beginning of the palps and ovigerous legs, show the common type of the beginning of legs in Arthropoda, and I think it impossible to interpret them as the reduction of the small, but powerful, well developed embryonal legs. In the drawing of *Pseudop. circularis* I have given the greater part of the ganglionic system with the four large ganglia of the body, the very small abdominal ganglion, and the large, foremost ganglion, i. e. the coalesced ganglia corresponding to the embryonal legs, or the nethermost pharyngeal ganglion, ganglion suboesophageum. By comparison with the same nethermost pharyngeal ganglion in the second larval stage, fig. 12, it is seen, how the same pairs of processes and appendages have changed, the processes having become rather smaller, while the appendages have become large, lengthened, tapering to a pair of nerve threads which I have been able to follow some way in the direction of the ovigerous legs. In *Pall. n. sp.*, finally, in which the fourth pair of ambulatory legs are very long, and which is of an appearance almost like the drawing I have given of *N. grossipes*, pl. I, fig. 26, the beginnings have not gone farther than to form a pair of semiglobular tubercles before the base of the first pair of ambulatory legs.

As already mentioned, Dohrn, Bau u. Entwickl. Arthrop. 1870, pl. VI, fig. 11—13, has given three stages of the development of the larva of *Ammothea* (*Achelia*), the last one belonging to our third larval stage. On the place of the imaginal fore limbs, not the embryonal legs, are here seen two pairs of short, stubby appendages which I, in accordance with Dohrn, consider as the beginning of the palps and ovigerous legs, that is to say, not as embryonal legs that, having been reduced, now again are growing and developing, but as the imaginal fore limbs that have arisen anew, and are originating in the way common in Arthropoda. To me, at all events, the theory of the new formation of these limbs is no make-shift, as Dohrn thinks[1]) it has been to Semper to enable him to homologize the Pycnogonida and the Arachnida, but I have arrived at my opinion by following the development; it has, however, for me also the value to diminish the difference between the number of legs in the thorax of the Arachnida and the Pycnogonida, which difference, according to what has been stated here, would only be as 6 to 5.

Systematism.

Before entering upon the systematic representation of the species of the Pycnogonida, I shall have to say some words concerning the place of these animals in the system of the Arthropoda upon the whole, a question I frequently have touched on in the preceding section. To give here a copious representation of all the different opinions that have been set forth with regard to this question, would only be of little use, even if it might afford some interest to see how these animals have been regarded, now as Crustacea, now as Arachnida, and at last have been referred neither to one nor the other of these two classes, but have been declared a particular, independent group, outside of all the four classes of the Arthropoda (Kingsley, Classif. Arthrop.), nay, have even by some authors been regarded as a particular, fifth class (Sars, Pycnogonidea), comp. also Ihle, Phylog. Pantop.[2]). I think that by the treating of the question of the position of the Pycnogonida in the system too small regard, or, most frequently, no regard at all has been paid to the developmental history. As important momenta of resemblance with regard to the Arachnida, I think we may point out: 1) The proboscis of the Pycnogonida, which is found in all real Arachnida, and, as in these, is only a process of the trunk cp. p. 19. 2) The development of the body into two chief divisions, a thorax and an abdomen, each with its particular limbs or beginnings of limbs. By considering the limbs of the Pycnogonida the authors have always, or almost always, started from the point that the typical

---

[1]) Dohrn, Pantop. Golf. Neap. 1881, p. 240, says of the theory of Semper: Dadurch aber ward er (o: Semper) genöthigt, für die dann später bei den Männchen, nach geraumer Latenz wirklich hervorsprossende Extremität III (i. e. the second pair of imaginal fore limbs, or the ovigerous legs) den Eierträger, auf den Nothbehelf der Neubildung zu verfallen, — womit dann eben die ganze, auf diese Auffassung begründete Homologisirung der Pycnogoniden mit den Arachniden Banquerott machte.

[2]) The here mentioned paper by Ihle seems to me upon the whole to be most of all a curiosity, a pregnant instance of what may be the result of the loosest systematizing without the slightest personal examination. As a specimen I shall cite the following passage: Als die Ahnen der Pantopoden betrachte ich die Myriopoden, erstens weil die letzteren die einzigen Tracheaten sind, welche abdominale Extremitäten besitzen, und zweitens, weil wenn wir die Arachnoideen und Crustaceen ausschliessen , die Myriopoden die einzig übrig bleibenden Tiere sind, von welchen wir die Pantopoden ableiten können, sodass wir fast notgedrungen die ersteren als die Vorfahren der letzteren betrachten müssen .... und von ersteren (o: Myriopoden) haben sich selbständig Pantopoden, Insekten und Arachnoideen abgetrennt (l. c. p. 606).

PYCNOGONIDA

number of homologous limbs in the Arachnida is six pairs, but in the Pycnogonida seven pairs. But, as I have already tried to show in the foregoing, the seven pairs of limbs in the latter animals are not all reciprocally homologous, and the typical number of pairs is not seven, but nine. Of these nine pairs of limbs especially the four last pairs, the ambulatory legs, are not at all homologous with the ambulatory legs of the Arachnida, but in all likelihood with the four pairs of small processes that have been pointed out in the abdomen of the Arachnid-embryo, cp. Balfour, Notes on the Development of the *Francina*, 1880, and Locy, Observations on the Development of *Agelena nævia*, 1886. Both the mentioned authors represent four pairs of distinct beginnings of limbs arising from the abdomen of an embryo of an *Agelena*, Balfour, l. c. pl. XIX. fig. 5—8 pp. or pp. 1—pp. 4, of *Ag. labyrinthica*, and Locy, l. c. pl. II—IV, fig. 7—11, 13—14, 20—21 pt. app. of an *Ag. nævia*. These beginnings which may reach a rather considerable length, are by Balfour called "provisional appendages", a name also adopted by Locy. On the other hand, I know of no instance of the genitals or their excretory ducts in any Arthropod being found in the thorax or the limbs of this part, as would be the result of the common interpretation of the ambulatory legs of the Pycnogonida. 3) Furthermore we find in the Pycnogonida an organ so decidedly of the Arachnid-type as the chelifori, with which also join 4) the embryonal byssus-glands, a homologon of the poison-glands of the Arachnida. The want of particular respiratory organs gives no information with regard to systematism, but it may be said to point to an origin or development from primitive, larve-like forms. 5) Finally the presence of auxiliary claws (i. e. real claws) is an important feature in the Arachnida in contradistinction to the Crustacea.

Relying on the points given in the foregoing, I think myself justified in classing the Pycnogonida among the Arachnida, as a group which with regard to the outer appearance is very much deviating, as it has also become very strange by a strong development of organs that in other Arachnida are only begun, or have been reduced, and upon the whole adopted to the life in the water, especially the sea.

When we next pass to the inner systematism of the Pycnogonida, or the consecutive order of the species, we shall first have to consider that the species, as far as they are known, form a close and united series of forms, so that there can be no question of dividing them into different groups, corresponding to the division into orders in the animal world in general, or in the Arthropoda in particular. Even if we should follow the common notion, and consider these animals as having their place outside the acknowledged four classes of Arthropoda, they would not for that reason become a fifth class of the same rank as the other classes, nor will it be necessary to divide them into a smaller or greater number of orders, suborders, families, subfamilies, genera, subgenera, species, and subspecies. Corresponding frames may of course easily be put up, and have partly been put up; but then when the animals are to be classed according to such frames, these frames soon appear to be quite artificial, as in us species may be placed as well at one place as at the other. Therefore we also see, how the same species is, by different authors, referred, now to one genus or family, now to another, or even to different so-called orders. The genera and families, of course, are still less decidedly fixed, but have got their position in a way and to an extent, unknown or inconceivable inside the class of Insects. We have common larval type and common larval development, as it has been shown in the section on of development, the orders and families that have been put up, have in reality only been based on the fact, whether the foremost limbs, as well the embryonal limbs as the imaginal limbs, continue the typical development, or their development is checked on an earlier or later stage, whether they go through a slighter or more marked retrograde development, or how long they are kept upon the whole. How small a systematic importance these foremost limbs have, may be seen, among other things, by the fact that a pair of these limbs may be kept in one sex, while it is thrown off in the other, and thus the reason of the keeping seems only to be purely biological; moreover the keeping or the throwing off takes place without producing or corresponding to any other difference in structure between the two sexes. To make such organs the base of the division into orders, seems to me very unfortunate, and it is only for want of better characteristics that I have used these limbs as family distinctions — in reality they are only of value as generic distinctions. Therefore I do not think it necessary to enter upon a detailed valuation of the orders that have been put up.

Among the different systems those of Wilson, Syn. Pycnog. New. Engl. 1878, and Hoek, Report Pycnog., 1881, and Nouv. étud. Pycnog. 1881, seem to me to be the best. The system of Wilson must be said to be well worked out, but on the other hand it is rather artificial, too much stress being laid upon characteristics taken from the auxiliary claws and the number of joints in the palps and the ovigerous legs. The system of Hoek in Report Pycnog. is merely a grouping of the genera without any real arranging of these genera inside the families. In his system in Nouv. étud. Pycnog. p. 106 the number of families has been reduced to four, and these four correspond to my system, as well with regard to the appellations as, chiefly, to the characterization, and the genera contained in each of them; it is however to be noted that the genus *Pallenopsis* has by Hoek been referred to *Phoxichilidæ*, but by me to *Nymphonidæ*. The genealogical table given by Hoek with its extremely problematic primitive form *Archipycnogonum*, I am not able to appreciate rightly.

The system I have used, is more particularly intended for the Pycnogonida brought home by the Ingolf expedition with the object of its also being able to comprise the new species.

I. Fam. **Nymphonidæ.**

Corpus manifeste in segmenta partitum.
Rostrum cylindricum, inflexibile, libratum vel nutans.
Chelifori expleti, chela instructi.
Palpi vel expleti, vel imminuti, vel deficientes.
Pedes oviferi in utroque sexu.

The trunk distinctly segmented.
The proboscis cylindrical, inflexible, horizontal, or directed obliquely downward.
The chelifori well developed (with chela).
The palps well developed, or rudimentary, or wanting.
Ovigerous legs present in both sexes.

As it will appear from the family-diagnosis, this family comprises the species belonging as well to *Nymphon* as to *Pallene*, that is to say, the families *Nymphonidæ* and *Pallenidæ* of Sars. An

essential reason for me to incorporate the two families has been the fact that *Pallenopsis* which is most closely related to the genus *Pallene*, shows, by the formation of its palps that it will not do to lay too much stress upon the presence or absence of these organs.

I.   Subfam. **Nymphonini**.

Palpi expleti, pluries partiti.
Palps well developed, with more joints.

1.   Gen. **Nymphon** (Fabr. 1794).

Nymphon, Wilson, Syn. Pycnog. New-Engl., 1878.
Chætonymphon, Sars, Pygnog. bor. arct., 1888, pro parte.
Boreonymphon, Sars, ibid.

The genus *Nymphon* with the limits which have been given to it here by Wilson, includes a great number of species that might naturally be distributed to several groups, but the differences seem to me to be too small to justify the division into more genera, or the separating of more or fewer species of the genus *Nymphon* of Wilson. The genera *Chætonymphon* and *Boreonymphon*, for inst., which have been separated by Sars, l.c. p. 352 and 354, seem to me too little characteristic to be taken as more than groups of species, and with regard to *N. macronyx* which has been referred to *Chætonymphon*, I think it even doubtful, if it might not more easily be placed among the species that Sars still keeps as the genus *Nymphon*.

The species of the genus, brought home by the Ingolf, may be arranged as shown in the following analytical table.

a. The trunk naked.
  (The fingers of the cheke (i. e. both the immovable and the movable finger) dentate.
  The auxiliary claws well developed).
  b.   The oculiferous tubercle pointed.

  1. N. grossipes Fabr.
  2. N. Sluiteri Hoek.

  b. b.   The oculiferous tubercle truncate.
      c.   The first tarsal joint shorter than the second.

  3. N. brevitarse Kr.

      c. c.   The first tarsal joint as long, or longer than the second.
          d.   The two last joints of the palps short and thick.
          (The claws short, powerful.
          The fingers of the cheke short).

  4. N. serratum G. O. Sars.
  5. N. megalops G. O. Sars.
  6. N. Sarsii n. sp.

          d. d.   The two last joints of the palps long, thin.
              e.   The claws short, powerful.

  7. N. Hoekii n. sp.
  8. N. Stroemii Kr.

c. c. The claws long, thin.
    f. The fingers of the chelæ short.
    f. f. The fingers of the chelæ long.

9. N. longitarse Kr.
10. N. Groenlandicum n. sp.
11. N. elegans Hans.
12. N. leptocheles G. O. Sars.
13. N. macrum Wils.

a. a. The trunk hairy.
    g. The fingers of the chelæ dentate.
        (The auxiliary claws well developed).
        h. The hair-covering spread, fine.
        h. h. The hair-covering dense, coarse.

14. N. macronyx G. O. Sars.
15. N. spinosum Goods.
16. N. tenellum G. O. Sars.

    g. g. The fingers of the chelæ simple, strongly arcuate.
        (The auxiliary claws rudimentary).

17. N. robustum Bell.

1. **Nymphon grossipes** Fabr.

Pycnogonum grossipes O. Fabricius, Faun. Groenl., 1870, p. 229.
Nymphon grossipes Kroyer, Kundsk. Pycnog., 1844, p. 108.
— — Idem, Gaimard, Voy. Scand. Lappon., 1849, pl. 36. Fig. 1, a-h.
— — Wilson, Syn. Pycnog. New-Engl., 1878, p. 20. Pl. VII. Fig. 1, a-q.
— — Hansen, Kara-Hav. Pycnog., 1886, p. 16. Tav. XVIII. Fig. 8, 8 a.
— — Sars, Pycnogonidea, 1891, p. 65. Pl. VI. Fig. 2, 2 a-i.
Nymphon mixtum Kroyer, Kundsk. Pycnog., 1844, p. 110.
— — Idem, Gaimard, Voy. Scand. Lapp., 1849, Pl. 35. Fig. 2, a-f.
— — Hansen, Fortegn. dansk. Pycnog., 1884, p. 649.
— — Idem, Zool. Dan., 1885, p. 128. Tab. VII. Fig. 19.
— — Sars, Pycnogonidea, 1891, p. 68. Pl. VI. Fig. 3, 3 a-i.

I cannot side with Sars in considering the N. mixtum of Kroyer as a good species, but must agree with Wilson in uniting N. grossipes and N. mixtum; perhaps I may also be allowed to point out that Hansen in his list of Danish Pycnogonida seems inclined to approve of such a union.

Occurrence. The Ingolf-stations 2, 31, 87, 95, 127 state it to be taken in the Davis Strait, the Denmark Strait, as well midway between Greenland and Iceland as nearer to the latter island, in the mouth of Bredebugt ; further also in the Greenland Sea, and finally as far south as the boundary of the Norwegian Sea midway between the Faröe Islands and Iceland. The depths were from 50–752 fathoms (Danish).

Further it is found at the Zoological Museum from many localities. When it has been called by other names than that of N. grossipes, the name in question has been added in a parenthesis.

5*

From the western coast of Greenland it is found from the following localities: Near Upernivik, 18 fath., stones with a few algæ (Fylla, Holm); the port of Sukkertoppen, 10 fath., stones with algæ (idem), between the mouth of Kvanefjord and Frederikshaab, 16 fath. (idem); between the rocks and islands outside of Frederikshaab, 10—25 fath. (idem); the straits at Igaussak (south of Frederikshaab), 14 fath. (idem); from the Davis Strait: 67° 4′ Lat. N. 54° 28′ Long. W., 32 fath., stones without algæ (idem); 66° 32′ Lat. N. 35° 31′ Long. W., 100 fath. (idem); (mixtum) 66° 16′ Lat. N. 26° 8′ Long. W. 33 fath., bottom temperature ÷ 1 (Wandel); 65° 35′ Lat. N. 54° 50′ Long. W., 80 fath. (Fylla , Holm); from the eastern coast of Greenland, in the Greenland Sea: 72° 26′ Lat. N. 19° 35′ Long. W. 105 fath. (Deichmann); 72° 53′ Lat. N. 20° 36′ Long. W., 96 fath. (idem); at Iceland, off Stykkesholm (H. Jónsson); in the Norwegian Sea, 63° 15′ Lat. N. 9° 35′ Long. W. 270 fath. (Wandel); (mixtum, the original specimen of Krøyer) Trondhjem-Fjord, south of Laxen, 15 fath.; in the channel between the Faröe Islands and the Shetland Islands 61° 23′ Lat. N. 5° 04′ Long. W. 225 fath. (Wandel).

Distribution. Here it is first to be pointed out that I have united N. grossipes and mixtum, so that the general reference to Sars, Pycnogonidea, 1891, here applies to both the species of Sars. After our conception of the species, N. grossipes should be known as one of the most widely spread Nymphon-species, from the Kara Sea, the Barents Sea, the seas round Greenland, and the eastern coast of North America towards the north, to the North Sea, nay, even into the Sound, towards the south. Accordingly the Ingolf-expedition has not increased the distributional area of the species.

2. Nymphon Sluiteri Hoek.

Nymphon Sluiteri Hoek, Pycnog. Willem Barents , 1881, p. 18. Pl. II. Fig. 30–34.

Hansen, Kara-Hav. Pycnog., 1886, p. 12. Tab. XVIII. Fig. 5, 5 a-b.

Sars, Pycnogonidea, 1891, p. 73. Pl. VII. Fig. 2, 2 a-g.

Hoek says of this species that its oculiferous tubercle is non valde exaltata apice truncata , l. c. p. 18, which on the following page is rendered by: it is not very elevated and rounded at the apex ; but as well Hansen who has examined some 40 specimens, as Sars who has examined a great many , and the present author have only seen specimens with very pointed oculiferous tubercles, so that, no doubt, the single specimen of Hoek has, as is also observed by Hansen, been defective with regard to the oculiferous tubercle; Hoek also says of it that the state of preservation of this specimen was not quite satisfactory , l. c. p. 19.

Occurrence. The Ingolf-stations are the following: 105, 116, 138, according to which it has been taken in the Norwegian Sea, from the Faröe Islands in the south in an almost straight line to Jan Mayen in the north; the depths were 371—762 fath.

Distribution. The species had hitherto only been found as far north as the Kara Sea, the Barents Sea, and midway between the Finmark and Beeren Eiland, at a depth of 20—60 fath., in a long distance of 160 fath., Sars, l. c. p. 75. By the Ingolf it has been taken considerably farther to the north until 63° 22′ Lat. N., and at somewhat greater depths, until 762 fath.

3. **Nymphon brevitarse** Kr.

Nymphon brevitarse Kroyer, Knudsk. Pycnog., 1844, p. 115.

— — Idem, Gaimard, Voy. Scand. Lappon., 1849, Pl. 36. Fig. 4, a-f.

— Sars, Pycnogonidea, 1891, p. 61. Pl. V. Fig. 3, 3 a-g.

Nymphon grossipes (Fabr.) Wilson, Syn. Pycnog. New-Engl., 1878, p. 491. p. p.

I cannot follow Wilson, when he not only incorporates the *N. mixtum* of Kroyer, but also the *N. brevitarse* of the same author into the species *N. grossipes* of O. Fabricius.

Occurrence. The Ingolf-stations are 95 and 96, in the middle of the Denmark Strait. The depths were 752 and 735 fath., and the bottom temperatures 2 ,1 and 1 ,2.

Distribution. The species was formerly only known from Greenland (Kroyer), and one specimen from the straits of Matotschkin Sharr, on a depth of only 10—15 fath.

4. **Nymphon serratum** G. O. Sars.

Nymphon serratum Sars, Crustac. Pycnog., 1880, p. 471.

— Hoek, Pycnog. Willem Barents., 1881, p. 16. Pl. I. Fig. 24—28, Pl. II. Fig. 29.

— — Hansen, Kara-Hav. Pycnog., 1886, p. 7. Tab. XVIII. Fig. 2, 2 a-c.

Sars, Pycnogonidea, 1891, p. 95. Pl. X. Fig. 2, 2 a-b.

Occurrence. The Ingolf-stations are 93, 94, and 127, the two first in the Denmark Strait, towards the coast of Greenland, the last one in the Greenland Sea, not far from the northern coast of Iceland. The depth was in the Denmark Strait 204 and 767 fath., in the Greenland Sea only 44 fath.

Further it is found at the Zoological Museum from the Davis Strait: 65° 35' Lat. N. 54 50' Long. W., 80 fath. (Fylla , Holm, and 66° 32' Lat. N. 55 34' Long. W., 100 fath. (idem).

Distribution. Sars, Pycnogonidea, 1891, p. 97, regards it as a genuine arctic species, from the sea between Beeren Eiland and Spitzbergen (Sars), the Barents Sea (Hoek), the Kara Sea and the Davis Strait (Hansen), to which the Ingolf thus adds the southmost parts of the Greenland Sea and the Denmark Strait.

5. **Nymphon megalops** G. O. Sars.

Nymphon megalops Sars, Prodr. Crustac. Pycnog., 1877, p. 366. n° 7.

— Idem, Pycnogonidea, 1891, p. 98. Pl. X. Fig. 3, 3 a-g.

Occurrence. The Ingolf-stations 93, 138, and 143 show it to be taken as well in the Denmark Strait as in the southern part of the Norwegian Sea, at the first station at a depth of 767 fath., while at the two last-named stations in the Norwegian Sea the depths were respectively 471 fath. and 388 fath.

Previous to the Ingolf expedition it was found at the Zoological Museum from a high degree of latitude in the Denmark Strait: 65° 39' Lat. N. 28° 26' Long. W., 553 fath., the bottom stones and shells

Dyra, Ryder, near Iceland, one Danish mile east of Seydisfjord, 135 fath., the bottom black ooze (Wandel), and in the Faröe-Shetland Channel, 61 23′ Lat. N. 5 01′ Long. W., 255 fath., bottom temperature o rid ent.

Distribution. Sars, Pycnogonidea, 1891, p. 100, regards this species as a genuine arctic form, found to the south till off Storeggen, 63 16′ Lat. N. The Ingolf carries it southward until 62 58′, and the collections of the Museum till 61 23′ Lat. N. that is to say, southeast of the Faröe Islands.

6. **Nymphon Sarsii** n. sp.

Tab. III. Fig. 1 6.

Junior (poris genitalibus nullis).

Corpus subrobustum.

Collum breve.

Tuber oculare sat altum, robustum, inerme; ocelli magni, rotundati, in lateribus contingentes, anteriores posterioribus paulo majores.

Segmentum caudale breviusculum, paulum curvatum atque nutans.

Chelifori sat graciles, scapo longiusculo, quam chela multo longiore; chela brevinscula, palma longinscula quam pollice paulo longiore.

Palpi breves, articulis binis ultimis crassis, longitudine subæqualibus, conjunctis longitudinem articuli tertii fere explentibus.

Pedes oviferi sat longi, ungue paucidentato.

Pedes gressorii breves, crassi, articulis tarsalibus subæqualibus, conjunctis tertiam partem longitudinis articuli alterius tibialis explentibus, articulo altero tarsali serie aculeorum longorum in duabus partibus marginis interioris instructo. Unguis brevis, crassiusculus, unguiculis auxiliaribus sat gracilibus, dimidiam longitudinem unguis fere explentibus.

Long. tota $0,6^{cm}$. Rostri $2,8^{mm}$. Corporis $5,3^{mm}$. Segmenti caudalis $1,5^{mm}$.

The trunk rather robust.

The neck short.

The oculiferous tubercle rather high, robust, rounded, without teeth; the ocelli large, round, touching each other at the sides, the foremost a little larger than the hindmost.

The caudal segment rather short, a little bent, and directed downward.

The chelifori rather slender, the scape somewhat long, much longer than the chela: the chela rather short, the palm somewhat lengthened, a little longer than the movable finger.

The palps short, the two last joints thick, of about equal length, both joints together about as long is the third joint.

The ovigerous legs rather long, the claw with only few teeth.

The ambulatory legs short, thick, the tarsal joints about equally long, taken together as long as one third of the second tibial joint; the second tarsal joint with a series of long thorns along the two thirds of the inner edge. The claw short, rather thick, with rather slender auxiliary claws of about half the length of the claw itself.

Total length 9,6ᵐᵐ. The proboscis 2,8ᵐᵐ. The trunk 5,3ᵐᵐ. The caudal segment 1,5ᵐᵐ.

This species resembles very much the following species, *N. Hoekii*, but is easily distinguished from it by the shape of the chelifori and palps, and the much longer caudal segment. Only one single specimen is known, which moreover is not quite full-grown.

Occurrence. The Ingolf-station 2; the locality the boundary between the Norwegian Sea and the Atlantic, midway between the Faröe Islands and Iceland, 63 4' Lat. N. 9° 22' Long. W.; the depth was 262 fath., the bottom clay and gravel, and the bottom temperature 5°3.

<h3 style="text-align:center">7. Nymphon Hoekii n. sp.</h3>
Tab. III. Fig. 7 – 13.
Junior (poris genitalibus nullis).

Corpus sat robustum.

Collum breve.

Tuber oculare sat altum, robustum, obtusum, inerme; ocelli sat magni, rotundati, in lateribus contingentes, anteriores posterioribus vix majores.

Segmentum caudale breve, crassiusculum, paulum sursum curvatum.

Chelifori crassiusculi, scapo brevi, quam chela breviore; chela longiuscula, palma breviuscula, quam pollice breviore.

Palpi breviusculi, articulis binis ultimis sat gracilibus, longitudine subæqualibus, conjunctis articulo tertio manifeste longioribus.

Pedes oviferi sat longi, ungue multidentato.

Pedes gressorii breves, crassiusculi, articulis tarsalibus longitudine subæqualibus, conjunctis dimidiam longitudinem articuli alterius tibialis non explentibus, articulo altero tarsali absque aculeis in margine interiore. Unguis brevis, crassiusculus, unguiculis auxiliaribus sat gracilibus, dimidiam longitudinem unguis vix explentibus.

Long. tota 8ᵐᵐ. Rostri 2,8ᵐᵐ. Corporis 5,3ᵐᵐ. Segmenti caudalis 1ᵐᵐ.

The trunk rather robust.

The neck short.

The oculiferous tubercle rather high, robust, rounded, without teeth; the ocelli rather large, round, touching each other at the sides, the foremost hardly larger than the hindmost.

The caudal segment short, somewhat thick, bent a little upward.

The chelifori rather thick, the scape short, shorter than the chela; the chela rather long, the palm somewhat short, shorter than the movable finger.

The palps somewhat short, the two last joints rather slender, of about equal length, both together distinctly longer than the third joint.

The ovigerous legs rather long, the claw with many teeth.

The ambulatory legs short, rather thick; the tarsal joints of about equal length, together not so long as half the second tibial joint; the second tarsal joint without thorns in the inner edge. The claw short, somewhat thick, with rather slender auxiliary claws, scarcely half as long as the claw itself.

Total length 8^{mm}. The proboscis 2,8^{mm}. The trunk 5,3^{mm}. The caudal segment 1^{mm}.

This species is very much like the preceding one, but belongs, by the structure of its palps, to another specific group. Only a couple of not full-grown specimens have been taken.

Occurrence. The Ingolf-station 95, in the middle of the Denmark Strait, 65°14 Lat. N. 30°30 Long W.; depth 752 fath., bottom temperature 2°,1.

8. Nymphon Stroemii Kr.

Nymphon Stroemii Kröyer, Kundsk. Pycnog., 1844, p. 111.
  Idem, Gaimard, Voy. Scand. Lappon., 1849, Pl. 35. Fig. 3, a-f.
  Wilson, Syn. Pycnog. New-Engl., 1878, p. 17. Pl. VI. Fig. 1, a-h.
  — Hansen, Kara-Hav. Pycnog., 1886, p. 9. Tab. XVIII. Fig. 3.
  — Sars, Pycnogonidea, 1891, p. 80. Pl. VIII. Fig. 2, 2 a-k. p. p.
Nymphon gracilipes Heller, Crust. Pycnog. Tunic., 1875, p. 40. Taf. IV. Fig. 15. Taf. V. Fig. 1-2.
  — Sars, Pycnogonidea, 1891, p. 83. Pl. VIII. Fig. 3, 3 a-g. p. p.

As Wilson and Hansen I also must acknowledge that I cannot keep distinct *N. Stroemii* and *N. gracilipes*; for even if it may frequently be easy enough decidedly to refer a specimen to one or the other of the two forms, the decision is still oftener very difficult or quite impossible, or we find an intermingling of the separating characteristics.

Occurrence. The Ingolf-stations are: 2, 3, 4, 29, 32, 35, 44, 87, and 106. The number of stations shows to be sure that this species has been taken very frequently, but outside of the south-most part of the Norwegian Sea, and a little way into the Atlantic, as also in the western part of the Davis Strait, it has only been taken once by the Ingolf in the Denmark Strait, at the mouth of Brededugt on Iceland. The depths were from 68–545 fath.

From the collections of the Zoological Museum I may add the following localities: the Davis Strait, 63°56 Lat. N. 52°12 Long. W., 130 fath. (Wandel); 65°27 Lat. N. 54°15 Long. W. (idem); 65°35 Lat. N. 54°56 Long. W., 80 fath. (Fylla 1884); the Denmark Strait, 65°39 Lat. N. 28°25 Long. W., 553 fath. (Fylla 1888); the Greenland Sea, 69°25 Lat. N. 20°1 Long. W., 167 fath. (Hayr; the west coast of Norway (the original specimen of Kröyer); the Skager Rack, close to the Norwegian coast, 275 fath. Joh. Petersen; the Skager Rack, the Skaw in S. S. E. 34 miles, 210 fath. (idem); the Cattegat (idem).

Distribution. Sars gives a different sphere of distribution for his two species, *N. Stroemii* and *N. gracilipes*, a more southern one for the former, lesser form, and a more northern one for the latter, somewhat larger species. The limit as to the independence of the species that might be found in this or that instance, loses to me much of its importance, when I find forms quite corresponding to the *N. Stroemii* of Sars so far north as 65 34', in the Davis Strait; on the other hand, however, I must acknowledge that most of the specimens that I after Sars temporarily determined as *N. Stroemii*, are from more southern stations (2, 3, 4, 35, 44, 67), while those that I determined as *N. gracilipes*, are from more northern ones (29, 32, 106). It is, however, a well known fact that many animals, for inst. among the Crustacea, in the higher latitudes by and by assume a somewhat different shape and especially a more considerable size; I shall only remind of so well known animals as *Gammarus locusta* and *Amathilla Sabinei*.

If *N. grossipes* be taken in a so wide conception as here, its distribution will be very considerable. From the arctic seas around Franz-Joseph Land (Heller), the Barents Sea (Hoek), the Kara Sea (Hansen), and off Grinnell Land (Miers) it stretches in the west down along the eastern coast of North America (Wilson), and in the east along the Finmark (Sars) into the Norwegian Sea, and a little into the Atlantic, as also through the North Sea along the eastern coast of England (Goodsir), and to the east quite into the Skager Rack and the Cattegat.

9. Nymphon longitarse Kr.

Nymphon longitarse Kroyer, Kundsk. Pycnog., 1844, p. 112.
— — Idem, Gaimard, Voy. Scand. Lappon., 1849, Pl. 36. Fig. 2 a-f.
— —. Wilson, Syn. Pycnog. New-Engl., 1878. p. 19. Pl. VII. Fig. 2, a-h.
— Sars, Pycnogonidea, 1891, p. 75. Pl. VII. Fig. 3, 3 a-h.

Occurrence. The Ingolf-station 29 gives it to be taken in the Davis Strait close to the western coast of Greenland, at a depth of 68 fath.

Further it is found at the Zoological Museum from the following localities: Baffin's Bay 72 40' Lat. N. 57 15' Long. W., 118 fath. (Fylla . Holm); 69° 54' Lat. N. 55° 34' Long. W., 50 fath. (idem), and from the Davis Strait, along the western coast of Greenland till Igaliko (K. J. V. Steenstrup), and Frederikshaab (Lundbeck).

Distribution. Sars, l. c. p. 78, states it as occurring at Greenland (that is the western coast, Kroyer), the Barents Sea (Hoek), the eastern coast of North America (Wilson), and the eastern coast of England (Hoek), as he also himself has it from the whole Norwegian coast and from the Kara Sea.

10. Nymphon Groenlandicum n. sp.
Pl. III. Fig. 14—22.

Corpus sat gracile.

Collum breviusculum.

Tuber oculare altum, obtusum, angulis acutis; ocelli permagni, subovales, subæquales, tum in medio tum in lateribus contingentes.

Segmentum caudale breviusculum, in obliquum erectum.

Chelifori sat longi, graciles, scapo quam chela longiore, chela longiuscula, palma quam pollice multo breviore.

P. palpat long., articulis binis ultimis gracilibus, conjunctis articulo tertio manifeste longioribus, articulo ultimo quam paenultimo multo breviore.

Pedes oviferi sat longi, ungue multidentato.

Pedes gressorii breviusculi, sat graciles, articulis tarsalibus conjunctis dimidiam longitudinem articuli alterius tibialis manifeste longioribus, articulo altero tarsali quam priore multo longiore, utroque serie aculeorum gracilium sat longorum in margine interiore instructo. Unguis longiusculus, crassiusculus, unguiculis auxiliaribus gracilibus, brevibus, non tertiam partem longitudinis unguis explentibus.

Long. tota 7,5'. Rostri 2,3ᵐᵐ. Corporis 4ᵐᵐ. Segmenti caudalis 1,2ᵐᵐ.

The trunk rather slender.

The neck somewhat short.

The oculiferous tubercle high, truncate, with sharp corners; the ocelli very large, almost oval, of about the same size, touching each other in the middle and at the sides.

The caudal segment somewhat short, directed obliquely upward.

The chelifori rather long, slender, the scape longer than the chela; the chela rather long, the palm much shorter than the movable finger.

The palps rather long, the two last joints slender, together distinctly longer than the third joint, the last joint much shorter than the last but one.

The ovigerous legs rather long, the claw with many teeth. Organ of sense, see fig. 20 a.

The ambulatory legs somewhat short, rather slender, the tarsal joints together distinctly longer than half the second tibial joint, the second tarsal joint much longer than the first one, both with a series of slender, rather long thorns in the inner edge. The claw somewhat long and thick with slender, short auxiliary claws, not reaching to a third part of the length of the claw itself. Total length 7,5ᵐᵐ. The proboscis 2,3ᵐᵐ. The trunk 4ᵐᵐ. The caudal segment 1,2ᵐᵐ.

Occurrence. The Ingolf-station 27, the Davis Strait, 64 54' Lat. N. 55 10' Long. W., 393 fath. soft, gray clay, numerous pebbles, mostly granite; bottom temperature 3 8. Numerous specimens.

11. **Nymphon elegans** Hans.

Nymphon elegans Hansen, Kara-Hav. Pycnog., 1886, p. 11. Tab. XVIII. Fig. 4, 4 a-d.
Sars, Pycnogonidea, 1891, p. 86. Pl. IX. Fig. 1, 1 a-g.

Occurrence. The Ingolf-stations 15, 116, 126, and 138 show it to be taken in the Denmark Strait, the Greenland Sea, and the western part of the Norwegian Sea from Jan Mayen some way to the south, at a depth from 293 471 fath.

From the collections of the Zoological Museum may be added: Baffin's Bay 72 40' Lat. N. 57 15 Long. W. 118 fath., the bottom clay without algæ (Fylla, Hohm); the Denmark Strait, 63 15' Lat. N. 28 26' Long. W. 270 fath. (Wandel); and the Norwegian Sea, 61 23' Lat. N. 1 21' Long. W., 505 fath.,

Distribution. The species is rather widely spread; it was first known from the Kara Sea (Hansen), but is found to the south far down in the Norwegian Sea, and to the west it has been taken quite up in the Baffin's Bay.

12. Nymphon leptocheles G. O. Sars.

Nymphon leptocheles Sars, Pycnog. bor. arct., 1888, p. 348.
Idem, Pycnogonidea, 1891, p. 78. Pl. VIII. Fig. 1, 1 a-i.

Occurrence. The Ingolf-stations are: 7, 36, and 138; accordingly it is taken in the southern part of the Atlantic, towards Iceland, and in the Davis Strait; the depths from 362 – 600 fath.

Distribution. The species had hitherto only been taken by Sars, chiefly along the western coast of Norway until Lofoden, and in the sea between the Finmark and Beeren Eiland, Pycnogonidea, 1891, p. 80, so that the Ingolf shows it to be considerably wider spread as well to the south as to the west.

13. Nymphon macrum Wils.

Nymphon macrum Wilson, Pycnog. New-Engl. Adjac. Wat., 1878, p. 487. Pl. IV. Fig. 21—23.
— Sars, Pycnogonidea. 1891, p. 89. Pl. IX. Fig. 2, 2 a-g.

Occurrence. The Ingolf-stations are: 25, 27, 32, 33, 35, 81, all in the Davis Strait and the northernmost part of the Atlantic, S. W. of Iceland. The depths were most frequently between 318 and 582 fath.

Previously it was found at the Zoological Museum from the Denmark Strait, 66 20' Lat. N., 25 12' Long. W., 96 fath. (Wandel).

Distribution. Sars thinks the species to be originally arctic, because, besides occurring between the Finmark and Beeren Eiland, it has also been taken at the eastern coast of North America (Wilson); with this statement agrees also its occurrence in the Denmark Strait and the Davis Strait, from where it has passed a little towards the south, into the Atlantic.

14. Nymphon macronyx G. O. Sars.

Nymphon macronyx Sars, Prodr. Crustac. Pycnog., 1877, p. 365. n 3.
Hansen, Kara-Hav. Pycnog., 1886, p. 13. Tab. XVIII. Fig. 6, 6 a-c.
Chaetonymphon macronyx Sars, Pycnogonidea, 1891, p. 111. Pl. XII. Fig. 2, 2 a-k.

Occurrence. The Ingolf-stations are: 2, 4, 101, 103, 105, 116, 138, 139, 140, 141, all situated inside the southern and western parts of the Norwegian Sea, from the Faröe Islands quite to Jan Mayen. The depths were 262 – 702 fath. It was found in great numbers, most frequently together with N. robustum.

Distribution. The species is found widely spread, from the Kara Sea down along the coast of Norway to the Faröe Islands, but hitherto it has not been taken farther west than the western part of the Norwegian Sea.

15. Nymphon spinosum Goods.

Nymphon spinosum Goodsir, Spec. Pycnog., 1842, p. 139, pl. 3. fig. 3.
Idem, Spec. Gen. Char. Arach. Crust., 1844, p. 3. pl. 1. fig. 17 18.
Chaetonymphon spinosum Sars, Pycnogonidea, 1891, p. 107. Pl. XI. Fig. 3, 3 a-i.
Nymphon hirtipes Bell, Account Crust., 1855, p. 403. Pl. XXXV. Fig. 3.
Wilson, Syn. Pycnog. New-Engl., 1878, p. 22. Pl. V. Fig. 2. Pl. VI. Fig 2 a-k.
Hansen, Kara-Hav. Pycnog., 1886, p. 5 (159).
Chaetonymphon hirtipes Sars, Pycnogonidea, 1891, p. 103. Pl. XI. Fig. 2, 2 a-k.

The species is somewhat variable, but I find no sufficient reason to divide the forms belonging hither into two species, as has been done by Sars, even if I have to acknowledge that most of the found and examined specimens tolerably well or decidedly can be said to belong either to the N. spinosum of Sars, or to his N. hirtipes, as these species are diagnosticated and described in his last, large, and excellent work. Perhaps I may also here be permitted to state my opinion that Sars may be said generally to be too much inclined to form new and many species and genera inside the Arthropoda, whether it be Crustacea or Pycnogonida, which for the rest have been studied and drawn by him in so excellent a manner. That such a different view of the species and the genus cannot be referred to a less successful representation in words or in figures, and that the dispute cannot be decided by original specimens , will already be shown by the circumstance, that our museum by the liberality of Professor Sars is possessed of several such critical specimens, that have been determined by him, and that nevertheless my uncertainty and doubt of the goodness of the species have not been removed.

Occurrence. The Ingolf-stations are: 4, 9, 15, 25, 27, 32, 35, 51, 53, 54, 78, 87, 93, 98, 127, 144. This great number of stations shows it to be a widely spread species, mostly, however, to the south, in the southern part of the Norwegian Sea, and the northern part of the Atlantic, and into the Denmark Strait to 66 18′ Lat. N.; also, however, in the Greenland Sea, a little north of Iceland, and in the Davis Strait to 65 57′ Lat. N. 55 30′ Long. W. The depths were mostly from ca. 300 to ca. 800 fath., in a few instances between ca. 70 and ca. 140 fath., and rarely the water was so low as 35 and 44 fath.

From the collections of the Zoological Museum the following stations may furthermore be added: the Davis Strait, 66 49′ Lat. N. 66 28′ Long. W., 285 fath. (Wandel); 66 32′ Lat. N. 55 34′ Long. W. 600 fath. (Fylla , Holm; 65 27′ Lat. N. 54 15′ Long. W., 670 fath. (Wandel); 64 57′ Lat. N. 55 14′ Long. W., 426 fath. (idem; the Denmark Strait, 64 42′ Lat. N. 27 13′ Long. W., 426 fath. (idem); 65 39′ Lat. N. 28 28′ Long. W., 553 fath. (Fylla , Ryder); the Greenland Sea in Scoresby Sound (Deichmann; the Grassland Bay in the Denmark Island, 5 fath. (Bay); Angmagsalik, 11 fath. (idem); 69 25′ Lat. L. 20 1′ Long. W., 107 fath. (idem; 71 21′ Lat. N. 8 25′ Long. W. 160 fath. (Deichmann); 72 25′ Lat. N. 19 33′ Long. W., 44 fath.(idem; 72 26′ Lat. N. 19 35′ Long. W., 105 fath.(idem); 72 53′ Lat. N. 20 36′ Long. W., 400 fath. (idem. Besides we have it from the Faröe-Shetland Channel 61 23′ Lat. N. 5 4′ Long. W., 500 fath. (Wandel), and from the Skager Rack, the Tromlinger to N. W. ½ N. 38 miles, 300 fath.

Distribution. The species is circumpolar, and besides it follows as well the American as the European shores far southward, thus being one of the most widely spread and most common Pycnogonida on deep water.

16. Nymphon tenellum G. O. Sars.

Nymphon tenellum Sars, Pycnog. bor. arct., 1888, p. 353.
  – Idem, Pycnogonidea, 1891, p. 109. Pl. XII. Fig. 1, 1 a-h.

Occurrence. The Ingolf-stations are: 7, 28, and 44, showing it to be found in the northern-most part of the Atlantic and in the south of the Davis Strait in depths from 420 to 600 fath.

Distribution. The species had hitherto only been found by Sars in the sea off the Fin-mark, and consequently this author took it to be a genuine arctic form; the three stations given here, carry the species much farther south and west, always on very deep water.

17. Nymphon robustum Bell.
Pl. III. Fig. 23—24.

Nymphon robustum Bell, Account Crust., 1855, p. 409. Pl. XXXV. Fig. 4.
Chaetonymphon robustum Sars, Pycnogonidea, 1891, p. 115. Pl. XII. Fig. 3, 3 a-d.
Nymphon hians Heller, Crust. Pycnog. Tunic., 1875, p. 41. Tab. V. Fig. 3 - 5.

The species varies very much, especially as to size; thus a grown male has measured 23^{mm}, and an unripe female 19,5^{mm}, while on the other hand grown males of 11^{mm} are not rarely met. These differences for a long time induced me to suppose two or more species to be hidden under the old N. robustum, and so I began to study the several small and large specimens in their mutual contrast, and thought in the armature of the fourth and fifth joints of the ovigerous legs of the male to have found a sure criterion. I had, however, soon to give up the thought of the systematic importance of this armature; but nevertheless I have partly rendered it here in pl. III, fig. 23 and 24, as it seemed to me to give a good idea of the powerful development and the different shapes and positions as-sumed by the bristles of the legs for the attaching of the eggs and young: it is, however, also to be remembered that N. robustum is likely to be the Pycnogonid, on the male of which the young are most firmly attached, and cling for the longest time.

Occurrence. The Ingolf-stations are: 3, 4, 15, 41, 101, 103, 105, 115, 116, 126, 138, 139, 140, 141, 143. According to this series of stations it has most frequently been taken in the west and south parts of the Norwegian Sea, and some way into the Atlantic; single specimens have been taken in the Greenland Sea and the Denmark Strait. The depths were mostly between 300 and 800 fath., only once below 100 fath. viz. 86 fath.

In the Zoological Museum it is found from the Greenland Sea: 70 26' Lat. N. (Deichmann); 72 26' Lat. N. 19 35' Long. W., 105 fath. (idem); 72 53' Lat. N. 20 36' Long. W., 96 fath. large stones (idem); Scoresby Sound 3 -25 fath. (idem); from the Davis Strait, 66 16' Lat. N. 25 20' Long. W., 327 the Winkel. Further we have it also farther south than the Ingolf-stations, viz. in the Faröe-Shetland Channel, 61 23' Lat. N. | 21' Long., 505 fath. idem.

Distribution. This species is widely spread, as well far to the north, from the arctic North America (Ball, Discovery Bay (Miers), Franz-Joseph Land (Heller), and in the Kara Sea (Hansen), as also so far to the southward as 60 Lat. N.

2. Gen. **Paranymphon** Caull.

Paranymphon Caullery, Pycnogonides, 1896.

Corpus glabrum.
Processus corporis perlongi.
Chelæ resupinatæ, subinermes.
Palpi septem-articulati.
Pedes oviferi octo-articulati, ungulati.
Pedes gressorii absque ungniculis auxiliaribus.

The trunk smooth.
The processes of the trunk very long.
The chela bent backwards, the teeth weak and few.
The palps seven-jointed.
The ovigerous legs eight-jointed, provided with claws.
The ambulatory legs without auxiliary claws.

Caullery, l. c. p. 361 has founded the genus on one single characteristic, viz. the number of joints in the palps, which number, however, is wrongly given as 6 instead of 7. As moreover no real diagnosis has been given either of the genus or the species, I have thought it necessary to give such, but also to point out that, only one species of the genus being known, it will be difficult always to determine, which characteristics are to be regarded as generic, and which as specific ones.

Paranymphon spinosum Caull.
Pl. IV. Fig. 20—28.

Paranymphon spinosum Caullery, Pycnogonides, 1896, p. 361. Pl. 12. Fig. 1 6.

Corpus subrobustum.
Processus corporis perlongi, admodum discreti, in cornua alta, acuta, erecta ad finem producti.
Rostrum breve, nutans.
Tuber oculare peraltum, gracile, attenuatum, recurvum, absque ocellis.
Segmentum caudale permagnum, altissimum, erectum, paulum curvatum.
Palpi breves, articulis quaternis ultimis brevibus, longitudine sensim decrescentibus.

Pedes oviferi breves; pars terminalis pedum lamellis paucis cultriformibus armata; unguis permagnus, dentibus paucis armatus.

Pedes gressorii breviusculi, articulo altero tarsali quam priore vix breviore. Unguis tenuis, simplex, dimidiam partem articuli alterius tarsalis superans.

Long. tota 2^{mm}. Rostri 0.25^{mm}. Corporis 1.75^{mm}. Segmenti caudalis 1.2^{mm}.

The trunk somewhat clumsy.

The side-processes of the trunk very long, much separated, with high, pointed, horn-shaped processes.

The proboscis short, directed obliquely downward.

The oculiferous tubercle very high, slender, bent backward, without ocelli.

The caudal segment very large, erect, a little curved.

The palps short, the four last joints short, by degrees decreasing in length.

The ovigerous legs short; the terminal part with few, knife-shaped leaves. The claw very large, with few teeth.

The ambulatory legs rather short, the second tarsal joint scarcely shorter than the first. The claw fine, without auxiliary claws, longer than half the length of the second tarsal joint.

Total length 2^{mm}. The proboscis 0.25^{mm}. The trunk 1.75^{mm}. The caudal segment 1.2^{mm}.

The habitus figure of Caullery is so rough and so bad, his characters as well of the genus as the species so poor, and besides, I think, partly useless or impossible, so that one is strongly tempted to pay no regard to the species here made by him; as, however, on the other hand, his species is so characteristical, and in several essential characteristics agree with the form represented here, I have thought the identity so probable that I have adopted his generic and specific name. Already before I have stated as my opinion that it is incorrect to give the palps 6 joints in stead of 7: as impossible I shall briefly mention another character. In his description of the species Caullery, l. c. p. 362, mentions some clavate bristles which are said to be found on the chelifori and the other limbs! His words run thus: Les mandibules portent (comme les autres appendices) des soies formées d'un axe rigide légèrement courbé, terminé en pointe et recouvert dans sa partie terminale d'un manchon verdâtre qui donne à l'ensemble une forme en massue. He moreover draws one of these bristles, not only in pl. 12, fig. 3 and 4, but also separately, more enlarged, fig. 6; but these formations are only common bristles with a bit of mud on the end, that is to say, pure products of art.

Occurrence. The Ingolf-stations are: 25 and 94. The former of these stations gives it as taken in the Davis Strait, 63 30' Lat. N. 54 25' Long. W., 582 fath.; the bottom was soft mud with a temperature of 3 3; about ten specimens were taken here; the latter station is in the Denmark Strait towards the eastern coast of Greenland 64 56' Lat. N. 36 19' Long., 204 fath., sand, the bottom temperature 4 1.

Distribution. This species was formerly only known from three specimens taken in three places in the Bay of Biscay on depths between 950—1700^m. The bottom was in all three places mud (vase), to which, of course, the mentioned and drawn wonderful bristles owed their knobs.

2. Subfam. **Pallenini**.

Palpi deficientes vel imminuti.

The palps wanting or rudimentary.

1. Gen. **Pallene** (Johnst.).

Pallene Wilson; Syn. Pycnog. New-Engl., 1878.
Sars, Pycnogonidea, 1891.

1. **Pallene acus** n. sp.

Pl. IV. Fig. 8—13.

Corpus subgracile.

Collum breve.

Rostrum crassum.

Tuber oculare altum, acutissimum, erectum, paulum curvatum, absque ocellis.

Segmentum caudale magnum, in obliquum erectum.

Pedes oviferi longi; pars terminalis pedum laminis latis, ovalibus 10—12 instructa.

Pedes gressorii longi, articulo altero tarsali in margine interiore acie angusta, longa instructo. Unguis permagnus, validus, quartas partes articuli alterius tarsalis fere explens, unguiculis auxiliaribus gracilibus, tertiam partem longitudinis unguis fere referentibus.

Long. tota 3^{mm}. Rostri 0,65^{mm}. Corporis 2,2^{mm}. Segmenti caudalis 0,5^{mm}.

The trunk rather slender.

The neck short.

The proboscis thick.

The oculiferous tubercle high, very pointed, erect, a little curved, without ocelli.

The caudal segment large, obliquely erect.

The ovigerous legs long; the terminal part with 10 to 12 broad, oval leaves.

The ambulatory legs long, the inner edge of the second tarsal joint with a long, narrow cutting-blade. The claw very large, powerful, about four fifths of the length of the second tarsal joint, with slender auxiliary claws, of about one third of the length of the claw.

Total length 3 — The proboscis 0,65^{mm}. The trunk 2,2^{mm}. The caudal segment 0,5^{mm}.

The cutting edge or blade-facies that in this species and the following one is mentioned as projecting from the inner margin of the second tarsal joint, corresponds to a similar formation on the same tarsal joint in *Phoxichilidium petiolatum*, which is drawn by Hansen, Zoolog. Dan., 1885, t. VII, fig. 22 c.c., and in the explanation of the figures, p. IX, called "a cutting edge on the lower margin of this", in the text, p. 130, it is called "a cutting ridge formed like the blade of a knife".

The same edge is later mentioned in the same Pycnogonid by Sars, Pycnogonidea, 1891, p. 26, as an undivided lamella , cp. pl. II, fig. 2 h. The edge is undivided, but in this species and the following one it is supported by a series of thickenings or ridges, running parallel and somewhat obliquely from the inner side outward, comp. my fig., pl. IV, fig. 13, and with regard to the following species fig. 18 and 19.

Occurrence. The Ingolf-station 24, in the Davis Strait, 63 06' Lat. N. 56 00' Long. W., 1199 fath.; the bottom bluish-gray, soft mud, the temperature 2 4. About ten specimens were taken here.

2. Pallene hastata n. sp.
Pl. IV. Fig. 14 19.

Corpus subgracile.

Collum longum.

Rostrum crassum.

Tuber oculare altum, acutissimum, erectum, paulum curvatum, absque ocellis.

Segmentum caudale breve, crassinsculum, in obliquum erectum.

Pedes oviferi longi; pars terminalis pedum laminis latis, ovalibus 10 11 instructa, in articulo tertio organum sensile (auditorium?) perspicuum; in margine articuli quarti exteriore setæ paucæ curvatæ (♂?).

Pedes gressorii longi, articulo altero tarsali in margine interiore acie angusta, longa instructo. Unguis magnus, validus, tres partes articuli alterius tarsalis fere explens, unguiculis auxiliaribus gracilibus, quintam partem longitudinis unguis fere explentibus.

Long. tota 3,7^{mm}. Rostri 0,84^{mm}. Corporis 2,5^{mm}. Segmenti caudalis 0,42^{mm}.

The trunk somewhat slender.

The neck long.

The proboscis thick.

The oculiferous tubercle high, extremely pointed, erect, a little curved, without ocelli.

The caudal segment short, somewhat thick, obliquely erect.

The ovigerous legs long, the terminal part with 10 to 11 broad, oval leaves; in the third joint is the organ of sense (ear?) transparent; in the outer edge of the fourth joint some few, curved bristles (♂?).

The ambulatory legs long, the inner edge of the second tarsal joint with a long, narrow cutting blade. The claw large, powerful, of about three fourths of the length of the second tarsal joint, with slender auxiliary claws of about one fifth of the length of the claw.

Total length 3,7^{mm}. The proboscis 0,84^{mm}. The trunk 2,5^{mm}. The caudal segment 0,42^{mm}.

With regard to the sensorium, fig. 17 a, I must refer to the foregoing.

Occurrence. The Ingolf-station 36 gives the species as taken in the southern part of the Davis Strait, 61 50' Lat. N. 56 21' Long. W., 1435 fath., the bottom gray mud, with a temperature of 1 5. About ten specimens were taken.

2. Gen. **Cordylochele** G. O. Sars, 1888.

Cordylochele Sars, Pycnog. bor. arct., 1888.

1. **Cordylochele malleolata** G. O. Sars.

Pallene malleolata Sars, Crust. Pycnog., 1880, p. 469.
Cordylochele malleolata Sars, Pycnogonidea, 1891, p. 45. Pl. IV. Fig. 1, 1 a-k.

Occurrence. The Ingolf-stations are: 4, 9, 32, 126, that is to say the southern part of the Norwegian Sea, the Greenland Sea, the Denmark Strait, and far up in the Davis Strait. The depths were between 200 and 300 fath.

Distribution. According to Sars, Pycnogonidea, 1891, p. 48, it is a genuine arctic form, from the Kara Sea, Spitzbergen, and Beeren Eiland. By the Ingolf it was taken somewhat farther south and west.

2. **Cordylochele longicollis** G. O. Sars.

Cordylochele longicollis Sars, Pycnog. bor. arct., 1888, p. 344.
— Idem, Pycnogonidea, 1891, p. 49. Pl. IV. Fig. 2, 2 a-g.

Occurrence. The Ingolf-stations 27 and 73 show it to be taken in the Davis Strait and in the Atlantic S.W. of Iceland. The depths were between 400 and 600 fath.

Distribution. Hitherto the species was only known from the coasts of Norway and Lofoden.

3. Gen. **Pseudopallene** Wils., 1878.

Pseudopallene Wilson, Syn. Pycnog. New-Engl., 1878, p. 10.

Pseudopallene circularis Goods.

Pallene circularis Goodsir, New spec. Pycnog., 1842, p. 137. pl. 3. fig. 2.
Pseudopallene circularis Sars, Pycnogonidea, 1891, p. 38. Pl. III. Fig. 3, 3 a-h.
Pallene intermedia Kröyer, Kundsk. Pycnog., 1844, p. 119 (full-grown).
Idem, Gaimard, Voy. Scand. Lappon., 1849, Pl. 37. Fig. 2, 2 a-l.
Pseudopallene intermedia Hansen, Kara-Hav. Pycnog., 1886, p. 21. Tab. XIX. Fig. 2, 2 a-l.
Pallene discoidea Kröyer, Kundsk. Pycnog., 1844, p. 120 (young).
Idem, Gaimard, Voy. Scand. Lappon., 1849, Pl. 37. Fig. 3, a-g.
Pseudopallene discoidea Wilson, Syn. Pycnog. New-Engl., 1878, p. 12. Pl. III. Fig. 3, a-b (young).
Pseudopallene hispida (Stimps.) Idem, Syn. Pycnog. New-Engl., 1878, p. 10. Pl. III. Fig. 1 a-e (full-grown).

Occurrence. The Ingolf-station 127, i. e. the Greenland Sea, North of Iceland, 66° 33' Lat. N. 15° Long. W. depth 44 fath.

Besides the stations mentioned by Hansen, l. c, p. 23, from the south-western coast of Nova Zembla, the western coast of Greenland, the Finmark, and Kullen, it is found in the Zoological Museum also from the Davis Strait 65 35′ Lat. N. 54 50′ Long. W., 80 fath. (idem); the belt of rocks and islands outside Frederikshaab, 25 fath. (idem, and Lundbeck); in the Bredebugt (the Denmark Strait) 9 fath. (the lieutenant Jensen); in the Ofjord (the Greenland Sea) 15 fath. (Diana).

Distribution. The species is one of the most widely spread Pycnogonida, from the arctic seas quite down into the Sound, and towards the west from the Davis Strait along the eastern coast of America; it keeps, however, mostly nearer to the coast, and the depths are most frequently small, rarely more than 100 fath.

3. Gen. **Pallenopsis** Wils., 1880.

Pallenopsis Wilson, Report Pycnog. Blake , 1880.

Pallenopsis plumipes n. sp.

Pl. IV. Fig. 1—7.

Corpus sat robustum, glabrum.

Collum vix ullum.

Rostrum longum, percrassum, obconicum, ante medium manifeste constrictum.

Tuber oculare parum altum, tumidum, apice obtuso, recurvo, tuberculis minimis scabroso; ocelli parvi rotundi, maculis pigmentariis permagnis.

Segmentum caudale gracillimum, productum, subcylindricum, ad apicem vix clavatum, in obliquum erectum.

Chelifori sat longi, graciles, scapo manifeste bipartito; digiti longiusculi, graciles, sat hiantes, inermes.

Palpi breves, solidi, acuminati.

Pedes oviferi breves, absque ungue; pars terminalis pedum absque laminis.

Pedes gressorii longi, longitudinem totam quater explentes, sat graciles, articulo priore tibiali pro parte, altero toto binis seriebus setarum longarum natatoriarum instructis. Unguis minus productus, sat gracilis, unguiculis auxiliaribus brevibus, gracillimis.

Long. tota 29^{mm}. Rostri 9^{mm}. Corporis 13^{mm}. Segmenti caudalis 7^{mm}.

The trunk rather plump, smooth.

The neck scarcely conspicuous.

The proboscis long, very thick, obconical, before the middle distinctly constricted.

The oculiferous tubercle not high, swollen, the point rounded, bent backwards, roughened by very small knobs; the ocelli very small, round, the coloured spots very large.

The caudal segment very slender, very long, almost cylindrical, slightly clavate towards the point, obliquely erect.

Palpi held on rather long, slender, the scape distinctly two-jointed, the fingers rather long, slender, somewhat gaping, without teeth.

The palps short, unjointed, tapering.

The ovigerous legs short, without claw; the terminal point without dermal leaves.

The ambulatory legs long, four times the total length, rather slender, the first tibial joint partly, the second one in the whole length provided with two series of long natatory bristles. The claw not very long, rather slender, with short, very slender auxiliary claws.

Total length 20^{mm}. The proboscis 9^{mm}. The trunk 13^{mm}. The caudal segment 7^{mm}.

Occurrence. The Ingolf-station 47, in the north-eastern Atlantic, 61° 32' Lat. N, 13° 40' Long. W, depth 950 fath. The bottom gray clay with Globigerina shells and a temperature of 3.23. One single female.

For elucidating the genus *Pallenopsis*, and the species of Kroyer *Pall. fluminensis* that has been much discussed, I shall here, relying on the original specimen of the museum, give some particulars, starting with a new diagnosis of the species.

Pallenopsis fluminensis Kr.
Pl. V. Fig. 1–6.

Phoxichilidium fluminense Kroyer, Kundsk. Pycnog., 1844, pp. 104 and 124. Tab. I. Fig. 1, a-f.

Hoek, Report Pycnog. Challenger, 1881, p. 81. Pl. XIV. Fig. 1-4.

Pallene fluminensis Semper, Pycnog. Larvenf., 1874, p. 282.

Bohm, Pycnog. Berl., 1879, p. 180, Tab. I. Fig. 4, 4 a-f.

Pallenopsis fluminensis Wilson, Report Pycnog. Blake, 1882, p. 250.

Schimkéwitsch, Pantop. Vettor Pisani, 1890, p. 14 (339), Fig. 24-31.

Corpus sat robustum, glabrum.

Colium perbreve.

Rostrum breviusculum, crassiusculum, in medio vix constrictum.

Tuber oculare sat altum, erectum, subconicum, ad apicem paulum attenuatum; ocelli perparvi, rotundi.

Segmentum caudale crassiusculum, minus productum, in obliquum erectum.

Chelifori breviusculi, sat robusti, scapo subsolido, aegerrime partito; digiti perbreves, crassi, vix hiantes.

Palpi perbreves, solidi, obtusi.

Pedes oviferi breves, absque ungue.

Pedes gressorii breviusculi, crassiusculi; ductus glandarius in articulo quarto maris brevis. Unguis sat longus atque robustus, unguiculis auxiliaris sat robustis, dimidiam longitudinem unguis paulum excedentibus.

Long. totius 7,1. Rostri 1,7^{mm}. Corporis 1,3^{mm}. Segmenti caudalis 2^{mm}.

The trunk rather clumsy, smooth.

The neck very short.

The proboscis very short and thick, scarcely constricted in the middle.

The oculiferous tubercle rather high, erect, almost conical, a little tapering to the top; the ocelli very small, round.

The caudal segment somewhat thick, not very long, obliquely erect.

The chelifori somewhat short, rather clumsy, the transverse partition of the scape scarcely visible; the fingers very short, scarcely gaping.

The palps especially short, unjointed, truncated.

The ovigerous legs short, without claws.

The ambulatory legs somewhat short and thick, the gland duct on the fourth tarsal joint of the male short. The claw rather short and clumsy, with rather clumsy auxiliary claws of a little more than half the length of the claw.

Total length $7,1^{mm}$. The proboscis $1,7^{mm}$. The trunk $4,3^{mm}$. The caudal segment 2^{mm}.

One single male taken in the port of Rio de Janeiro, and brought home by Kroyer; it is still found in the museum.

Kroyer, l. c. pp. 104 and 124, established this species as a *Phoxichilidium*, and gave also drawings of the animal, as well as some particulars; but Kroyer was no skilful drawer, and in this instance he was especially unfortunate; and as, moreover, Kroyer, contrary to his common accuracy, has made some essential errors by failing to see, it will be understood, that uncertainty might easily arise as to the interpreting of this species of his. It will therefore be of some interest to get a new description of the species, and it is only to be regretted that the original specimen has been treated so badly by being used for representation. That notwithstanding the errors and representation of Kroyer the divinations hitherto seem to have been correct, will not be of any importance so as to prevent a future author in putting up (and, as it would seem, in rightly doing so) the species of Kroyer as a type of a new genus.

Kroyer, as we have seen, referred the species to the *Phoxichilidium* of Milne-Edwards, of which genus he, l. c. p. 121, gave a copious description in Latin, which description was to comprise all the species of the genus known to him. In this description the chelifori are mentioned in the following manner: Mandibulae .... maximae sunt (dimidiam animalis longitudinem fere aequantes), ex articulo compositae basali, chelaque breviore — accordingly only one joint in the scape. Of the palps it is said: Maxillae prioris paris desunt — accordingly the palps are wanting. From the specific description may be pointed out that the ovigerous legs, l. c. p. 124, are said to be tenjointed, from which the inference may be drawn that the animal has been full-grown, and further it may be noticed that the bristles on the ambulatory legs are not mentioned, from which fact we may securely conclude that the specimen of Kroyer has had no specially conspicuous bristles, or, at all events, that Kroyer has not observed this peculiarity which was otherwise well known to him, and which he has often mentioned and described in the sea-Arthropoda examined by him. (I have in vain searched for such feathery bristles, comp. Bohm l. c. p. 182, Pl. I, fig. 4 f). Finally Kroyer has not mention , m of less drawn the gland ducts (ductus glandarii), really found in his original specimen. With regard to the figures it has to be pointed out that neither in fig. 1 a nor in fig 1 b of Kroyer does the scape of the chelifori show any sign of articulation, and that only in the middle of the scape in fig. 1 c a slight swelling is found. Further it must also be noticed that, while in the text, l. c. p. 106, Kroyer gives the longitudinal relation between the fourth, fifth, and sixth joints of the ambulatory legs as $1, 2,$ and $3,$ this ratio is in fig. 1 f as $27, 27,$ and $24.$

According to what has been stated here, I think that Semper, who has nothing but the representation by Kroyer to rely on, has been very bold in referring *Phoxichil. fluminense* to the genus *Pallene*, l. c. p. 282. Neither do I think that Bohm has been justified in referring some Pycnogonids, although they have been taken at the coasts of South America, to the *Phoxichil. fluminense* of Kroyer, at the same time referring this species to *Pallene* Johnst. The species described and drawn under this appellation by Bohm, may as well be a genuine *Pallene* Wils., with the scape of the chelifori undivided, and no gland duct on the ambulatory legs of the male; and even if Bohm, contrary to the description of Kroyer, might regard *Phoxichil. fluminense* as a *Pallene*, the ratio between the joints of the ambulatory legs is so different from the statements of Kroyer (whether regarding his text or his figures), and the presence or absence of feathery bristles is so important a feature, that Bohm ought to have hesitated very much in identifying the species. Hoek draws and describes a *Phoxichil. fluminense* Kr. that no doubt belongs to the genus *Pallenopsis* Wils., and is nearly related to *fluminense*, but the description is insufficient, and the figures, especially that of the oculiferous tubercle, fig. 2, so unlike the real *Pall. fluminensis*, that very possibly it may be another species.

Wilson, l. c. p. 250, refers as well the species of Kroyer as that of Bohm to his new genus *Pallenopsis*, without, as it seems, to be quite clear of the uncertainty, but nevertheless I suppose that his genus also comprises *Phox. fluminense*, although this latter in the one rather essential point that by Wilson is regarded as the chief point, that is to say, the construction of the scape of the chelifori, deviates from the characteristics of the new genus. The description and figures of Schimkéwitsch are, like those of Hoek, insufficient, and especially the highly developed bristles, fig. 28 and 29, might indicate another species.

According to the preceding, as well Semper as Bohm and Wilson seem to have referred the *Phox. fluminense* of Kroyer correctly to the genera known and acknowledged by them, although none of them have seen the original specimen of Kroyer, and notwithstanding the fact, that the representation by Kroyer is not only incomplete, but even incorrect in several, and in some of the most essential, points. On the contrary I think the species of Bohm to be different from that of Kroyer, and likewise I think it very uncertain that Hoek and Schimkéwitsch have had the species of Kroyer.

II. Fam. Ascorhynchidæ.

Corpus plus vel minus manifeste in segmenta partitum.
Rostrum tumidum, plus vel minus flexibile.

Chelifori incompleti, chela plus vel minus inminuta.
Palpi expleti.
Pedes oviferi in utroque sexu.

The trunk more or less distinctly segmented.
The proboscis swollen, more or less movably articulated.
The chelifori defectively developed, the chela more or less rudimentary.
The palps well developed.
Ovigerous legs present in both sexes.

Gen. **Ascorhynchus** G. O. Sars.

Ascorhynchus Sars. Prodr. Crust. Pycnog., 1877.

Referring in all essentials to the generic diagnosis of Sars, such as he has given it in his principal work on the Pycnogonids, Pycnogonidea, 1891, p. 132, I must, however, on account of an observation by the examination of these animals, wish to have it altered a little. By examining a full-grown female I found that this specimen had long fingers with an equal development of both; the whole chela, however, was somewhat shrivelled, and the fingers relatively much thinner, not only than in other Pycnogonida, but also thinner than in earlier stages of the same species, so that the whole chela gets a somewhat rudimentary appearance, cp. my figure, pl. V, fig. 13. This observation also influences the family-diagnosis.

Ascorhynchus tridens n. sp.
Pl. V. Fig. 7—18.

Corpus sat gracile, marginibus posticis annulorum corporis ipsis in apicem productis.
Collum sat breve.
Rostrum crassum, manifeste restrictum.
Tuber oculare magnum, apice in angulum producto, dentibus lateralibus acutis.
Segmentum caudale gracile, libratum.
Chelifori breves; digiti saepissime inminuti, interdum producti, graciles.
Palpi longiusculi. Organum sensile manifestum.
Pedes oviferi longiusculi, laminis partis terminalis pedum ad basin in dentes senos magnos incisis.
Pedes gressorii breviusculi, scabrosi, dense hirti, articulo priore tarsali quam altero ter breviore, articulo altero minus dense pectinato, articulo quarto pedum trium parium posteriorum solummodo nodulo armato.
Long. tota (rostro porrecto) 10^{mm}. Rostri 4^{mm}. Corporis 5^{mm}. Segmenti caudalis 1,6^{mm}.

The trunk rather slender, the posterior edge of the rings produced into a pointed tooth.

The neck rather short.

The proboscis thick, distinctly constricted.

The oculiferous tubercle large, the apex produced into an angle, the side-teeth sharp.

The caudal segment slender, perpendicularly erect.

The chelifori short; the fingers mostly rudimentary, sometimes long, slender.

The palps somewhat long. Sensory distinct.

The ovigerous legs somewhat long; the dermal leaves of the terminal part with 6 strong teeth at the base.

The ambulatory legs somewhat short, rough, densely hairy, the first tarsal joint three times shorter than the second one, the comb of the second joint less small-toothed, only the fourth joint of the three hindmost pairs of legs with a tubercle.

Total length (with the proboscis produced) 16^{mm}. The proboscis 4^{mm}. The trunk 5^{mm}. The caudal segment 1.6^{mm}.

This species is very much like *Ascorhynchus abyssi* of Sars Pycnogonidea, 1891. p. 133, pl. XIV, fig. 2, 2 a-t, and I was long doubtful whether I should set it up as a particular species. Among the characters of the diagnosis I may especially point to the shape of the oculiferous tubercle, having always found its dorsal side produced in the middle to an acute angle with sharp teeth on the sides. The neck is also much shorter, the point of the rings of the trunk is drawn back quite to the posterior edge, the caudal segment is horizontal, not directed downward, and the armament of the inner edge of the second tarsal joint is much more spread than in *Ascorhynchus abyssi*. I have also pointed out that the sensory in the palps is distinctly discernible, and that only the three hindmost pairs of ambulatory legs have the tubercle on the fourth joint, already represented by Sars; but it is possible or probable that these two characters may be found also in *Ascorhynchus abyssi*. Finally the ratio of length between the joints of the palps is not a little different from that in the species of Sars. The differing structure of the chela and its fingers is scarcely to be regarded as a specific character.

Occurrence. The Ingolf-stations 112, 113 and 124 are in the western part of the Norwegian Sea and in the southeastern part of the Greenland Sea. The two first places, on which it was taken in considerable numbers, were on 67° 57' Lat. N. 6° 44' Long. W., and 69° 31' Lat. N. 7° 06' Long. W., the depths were 1267 and 1309 fath., and the bottom was on both places Biloculina clay with temperatures of ÷ 1.1 and ÷ 1. On the third place, 67° 40' Lat. N. 15° 40' Long. W. the depth was only 135 fath., the bottom brownish gray, or blue mud or clay (not Biloculina clay) with short, cylindrical, tubulous foraminifera, and with a temperature of ÷ 0.6.

III. Fam. **Colossendeidæ.**

Colossendeidæ.

Proboscis validum, inflexibile, tubatum vel nutans.

Chelifori deficientes (in larvis interdum chelifori scapo bipartito præditi).

Palpi expleti.

Pedes oviferi in utroque sexu.

The trunk not divided into segments.

The proboscis colossal, inflexible, horizontal, or directed obliquely downward.

Chelifori wanting (in the larvæ sometimes chelifori with two-jointed scape).

The palps well developed.

Ovigerous legs present in both sexes.

Gen. Colossendeis Jarz. 1870.

Colossendeis Jarzynsky, Præm. cat. Pycnog., 1870.

1 Colossendeis proboscidea Sab.

Phoxichilus proboscideus Sabine, Mar. invert. anim., 1824, p. CCXXVI.

Colossendeis proboscidea Hoek, Pycnog. Willem Barents , 1881, p. 22. Pl. II. Fig. 41-42.

Hansen, Kara-Hav. Pycnog., 1886, p. 20.

— Sars, Pycnogonidea, 1891, p. 138. Pl. XV. Fig. 1, 1 a-d.

Colossendeis borealis Jarzynsky, Præm. cat. Pycnog., 1870.

Anomorhynchus Smithii Miers, Coll. Crust. Pycnog., 1881, p. 50. Pl. VII. Fig. 6-8.

Occurrence. The Ingolf-stations 116, 124 and 139 are from the western side of the Norwegian Sea up towards Jan Mayen and down towards the Faröe Islands, as also in the southern part of the Greenland Sea; the depths were 100--700 fath., and the bottom mud.

From the collections of the Zoological Museum may be added: the Davis Strait, 65° 27′ Lat. N. 54° 45′ Long. W., 67 fath., coral sand (Wandel), and the Norwegian Sea, off Lodmundarfjord, Snurrevaad> (a kind of fishing net used by Danish fishers for the fishing of plaice, by which a fishing ground is searched all round) (Diana , Horring).

Distribution. The species is likely to be circumpolar, widely spread; it seems to have been taken in the greatest number in the Kara Sea, reaching, however, down to 60° Lat. N.

2. Colossendeis clavata n. sp.

Pl. V. Fig. 19—20.

Corpus gracile.

Rostrum longum, crassum, bis inflatum.

Tuber oculare sat altum, ante præceps, post declive; ocelli anteriores magni, pyriformes, posteriores perparvi, ovales, cum margine posteriore ocellorum anteriorum emarginato contigui.

Segmentum caudale longum, clavatum.

Palpi breviusculi.

Pedes ovigeri breves.

Pedes gressorii subgraciles, longi, articulo priore tarsali quam altero duplo longiore. Unguis parvus, dimidiam longitudinem articuli alterius tarsalis vix excedens.

Long. tota 18ᵐᵐ. Rostri 24ᵐᵐ. Corporis 18,5ᵐᵐ. Segmenti caudalis 5ᵐᵐ.

The trunk slender.

The proboscis long, thick, swollen in two places.

The oculiferous tubercle rather high, anteriorly steep, posteriorly sloping; the foremost ocelli large, pyriform, the hindmost ones very small, oval, lying close to the emarginate hinder edge of the foremost eyes.

The caudal segment long, clavate.

The palps somewhat short.

The ovigerous legs short.

The ambulatory legs somewhat slender, long, the first tarsal joint twice the length of the second one. The claw small, scarcely exceeding half the length of the second tarsal joint.

Total length 18ᵐᵐ. The proboscis 24ᵐᵐ. The trunk 18,5ᵐᵐ. The caudal segment 5ᵐᵐ.

Occurrence. The Ingolf-station 64, that is the northern Atlantic south of Iceland, 62° 06′ Lat. N. 19° 05′ Long. W., 1041 fath. Bottom temperature 3 1. Only one single specimen, a full-grown female.

3. Colossendeis colossea Wils.

Colossendeis colossea Wilson, Report Pycnog. Blake, 1881, p. 244. Pl. I. Fig. 1. Pl. III. Fig. 5–7.
? Colossendeis gigas Hoek, Report Pycnog. Challenger, 1881, p. 61. Pl. VIII. Fig. 1—2. Pl. X. Fig. 1 5.
Nec! Colossendeis gigas (Hoek) Schimkéwitsch, Compte-rendu Pantop. Albatross, 1893, p. 29.

I suppose the *Colossendeis colossea* of Wilson to be different from the *Colossendeis gigas* of Hoek, and still more decidedly different from the species of the same name of Schimkéwitsch.

Occurrence. The Ingolf-stations are 11 and 18, the former being in the Denmark Strait, 63° 31′ Lat. N. 30° 12′ Long. W., 1300 fath.; the latter in the Atlantic, 61° 44′ Lat. N. 30° 29′ Long. W., 1135 fath. Three specimens were taken, the largest of which of a length of 63ᵐᵐ.

Distribution. Wilson has this species from the eastern coast of North America, from 41° 33′ Lat. N. to 38° 15′ Lat. N., and from 65° 47′ 10″ Long. W. to 73° 10′ 30″ Long. W. from depths between 524 1186 fath. According to my conception of the species this species is only known from the Ingolf, and the places stated by Wilson.

4. **Colossendeis angusta** G. O. Sars.

Colossendeis angusta Sars, Prodr. Crust. Pycnog., 1877, p. 368 n 8.

    —   Wilson, Report Pycnog. Blake , 1881, p. 243. Pl. III. Fig. 8 og 13.

    —   Hoek, Pycnog. Faroe Chann. Triton , 1884, p. 5. Pl. 1. Fig. 8.

                Hansen, Kara-Hav. Pycnog., 1886, p. 21.

    —   Sars, Pycnogonidea, 1891, p. 140. Pl. XV. Fig. 2, 2 a-f.

Nec! Colossendeis gracilis Hoek, Report Pycnog. Challenger , 1881, p. 69. Pl. IX. Fig. 6 — 8. Pl. X. Fig. 6 — 7.

    —   —   Schimkéwitsch, Compte-rendu Pantop. Albatross , 1893. p. 32.

I am decidedly of the opinion that the *Col. gracilis* of Hoek and the present species are different, even if by the mutual ratio of the last joints of the palps and by the specially long claws of the ambulatory legs they form a particular generic group. It is upon the whole only in the imago, or a far advanced stage of the development that the last joint but two of the palps assumes its peculiar shape, while in the very young larva the same joint, cp. fig. 22, does not deviate as to shape and position, but only as to length from the rule.

The chelifori found by Hoek in a couple of specimens of *Col. angusta* and *gracilis*, and by him mentioned as something quite strange or abnormal, I have found in upwards of a score of grown young ones (of a length of 13—14^{mm}) of *Col. angusta*, fig. 21, so that I should even be inclined to suppose that the young one as a rule keeps these larval limbs, until they are thrown off at the last moulting, cp. fig. 21. Also in a much younger larva (6^{mm} long) I have found chelifori of about the length of the proboscis, and with the scape divided into two distinct joints as in the full-grown larva. The fact of the scape being two-jointed seems to me to be of importance with regard to the characterization and systematic position of the family, and therefore I have also pointed out this feature in the family-diagnosis. Cp. also the essays by Hoek cited here.

Occurrence. The Ingolf-stations are 2, 3, 4, 64, 70, 103, 104, 105, 106, 110, 113, 117, 120, 125, 138, 140, 141. From the great number of stations it will be seen that this species not only without comparison has been the *Colossendeis* most frequently found, but also that in this respect it is inferior to no other Pycnogonid. It is especially in the southern part of the Norwegian Sea near the Faröe Islands, just at the boundary of the Atlantic that it has been found; it has, however, also been taken farther north in the same seas towards Jan Mayen, and one single specimen has been taken some way up in the Greenland Sea, stat. 125, 68 08' Lat. N. 16 02' Long. W. A few stations are also found in the Atlantic south of Iceland, stat. 64, 62 06' Lat. N. 19 00' Long. W. with a depth of 1041 fath. The depths were otherwise varying between 134 and 1309 fath., most frequently some 7—800 fath.

Distribution. From the Kara Sea (Hansen) and N. W. of Beeren Eiland (Sars) it is spread especially to the south in the Norwegian Sea and the Faröe-Shetland Channel (Hoek), and from there sparsely round the southern coast of Iceland to the eastern coast of North America (Wilson).

5. **Colossendeis macerrima** Wils.

Colossendeis macerrima Wilson, Report Pycnog. Blake , 1881, p. 246.
Pl. I. Fig. 2. Pl. III. Fig. 9 12. Pl. V. Fig. 32.

Occurrence. The Ingolf-stations 11 and 88 are in the Denmark Strait, partly midway between Greenland and Iceland, partly in the mouth of Bredebugt in the latter island. The depths were 1300 and 76 fath. Only two specimens were taken of which one, from Bredebugt, was a little young (without chelifori).

Distribution. The species had until then only been taken in one single specimen on 38 18' 40" Lat. N. 73 18' 10" Long. W. at a depth of 922 fath. (Wilson).

IV. Fam. Phoxichilidæ.

Corpus manifeste in segmenta partitum.
Rostrum cylindricum vel conicum, inflexibile, libratum vel nutans.
Chelifori vel robustiores, vel graciliores, vel deficientes.
Palpi deficientes.
Pedes oviferi in femina deficientes.

The trunk distinctly segmented.
The proboscis cylindrical or conical, inflexible, horizontal or directed obliquely downward.
The chelifori powerful, or slender, or wanting.
Palps wanting.
Ovigerous legs wanting in the female.

2. Subfam. Pycnogonini.

Chelifori deficientes.

Chelifori wanting.

Gen. Pycnogonum (Brünn. 1764).

Pycnogonum Wilson, Syn. Pycnog. New-Engl., 1878.

Pycnogonum crassirostre G. O. Sars.

Pycnogonum crassirostre Sars, Pycnog. bor. arct., 1888, p. 340.

— Idem, Pycnogonidea, 1891, p. 12. Pl. I. Fig. 2, 2 a-h.

Occurrence. The Ingolf-Station 88 is in the Denmark Strait in the month of Bredebugt in Iceland, at a depth of 76 fath., bottom temperature 6°9. One single male.

Distribution. Sars, Pycnogonidea, 1891, p. 14, could for his three specimens give no nearer determination than close to the coast of Norway, adding, however, from our museum a station in the Denmark Strait, off Dyrafjord in Iceland (Ryder). I should be inclined to think that the species keeps close to the coasts on not too deep water.

LIST OF LITERATURE.

Adlerz, G.: Bidrag till Pantopodernas Morfologi och Utvecklingshistoria.
Bih. t. K. Svenska Vet.-Akad. Handl. B. 13. Afd. IV. Nr. 11. Tafl. I—II. 1888.

Balfour, F. M.: Notes on the Development of the Araneina.
Quaterl. Journ. Microsc. Sc. New Ser. Vol. 20. p. 167–89. Pl. XIX—XXI. 1880.

Bell, Th.: Account of the Crustacea.
Last of the arct. voy. und. the Comm. of Capt. Sir Edw. Belcher in search of Sir John Franklin
dur. the years 1852—53—54. II. 1855.

Brünnich e, M. Th.: Entomologia sistens Insectorum Tabulas Systematicas cum Introductione et
Iconibus. Insektlære, indeholdende Insekternes systematiske Tavler samt Indledning og Fi-
gurer. 1764.

Bohm, R.: Ueber die Pycnogoniden des Königl. Zoologischen Museums zu Berlin, insbesondere über
die von S. M. S. Gazelle mitgebrachten Arten.
Monatsber. kön. preuss. Akad. d. Wiss. zu Berlin, aus d. Jahre 1879. p. 170—195. Taf. I—II. 1880.

Caullery, Maur.: Pycnogonides.
Résult. scient. d. l. Campagne du Caudan dans le Golfe d. Gascogne. Août-Sept. 1895. Fasc. II.
p. 361—64. Pl. 12. 1896.

Cavanna, G.: Studi e ricerche sui Pienogonidi.
Publicaz. del r. istit. di super. prat. e di perfez. in Firenze. Sez. di scienze fis. e natur. p. 3—19.
Tav. I—II. 1877.

Dohrn, A.: Untersuchungen über Bau und Entwicklung der Arthropoden.
Jenaische Zeitschr. f. Medic. u. Naturw. V. p. 138—57. Tab. V—VI. 1870.

Die Pantopoden des Golfes von Neapel und der angrenzenden Meeres-Abschnitte.
Fauna u. Flora d. Golf. v. Neap. u. d. angr. Meer.-Absch. herausgeg. v. d. Zool. Stat. zu Neapel.
III. Monographie. p. 1—252. Taf. I—XXII. 1781.

Fabricius, O.: Fauna Groenlandica. 1780.

Goodsir, H.: Description of some new species of Pycnogonidæ.
Jamesons Edinb. Phil. Journ. XXXII. 1842.

On the Specific and Generic Characters of the Araneiform Crustacea.
The Ann. and Mag. of Natur. Hist. Vol. XIV. p. 1—4. Pl. I. 1844.

Grassi, B.: Intorno ad un nuovo Aracnide artrogastro (Koenenia mirabilis), che crediamo rappresentante d'un nuovo ordine (Microteliphonida). Estr. dal Natural. Sicil. Anno IV. p. 1—14. 1885.

I Progenitori dei Miriapodi e degli Insetti. Memorie V. Intorno ad un nuovo Aracnide artrogastro Koenenia mirabilis rappresentante di un nuovo ordine (Microtelyphonida).
Bull Soc. Entom. Ital. Anno XVIII. p. 153—72. Tav. IX—X. 1886.

Hansen, H. J.: Fortegnelse over de hidtil i de danske Have fundne Pycnogonider eller Søspindler.
Naturh. Tidsskr. 3. R. 14. B. p. 617—52. 1884.

Hansen, H. J.: Zoologia Danica, Afbildninger af danske Dyr med populær Text. H. 4. 1885.
— Kara-Havets Pycnogonider.
    Dijmphna-Togtets zoologisk-botaniske Udbytte. p. 3—27. (157—81). Tab. XVIII—XIX. 1886.
Hansen, H. J. og Sorensen, Will.: The Order Palpigradi Thor. (Koenenia mirabilis Grassi) and
    its Relationship to the other Arachnida.
        Entom. Tidskr. Arg. 18. H. 3—4. p. 223—40. Tafl. IV. 1897. 1898.
Heller, Cam.: Die Crustaceen, Pycnogoniden und Tunicaten des K. K. Oester. Ungar. Nordpol-
    Expedition 1875.
        Denkschr. d. kais. Akad. d. Wiss. in Wien. Math.-naturw. Cl. Bd. 35. 1878.
Hoek, P. P. C.: Ueber Pycnogoniden.
        Niederl. Arch. f. Zool. 3. Bd. p. 1—20. Taf. XV—XVI. Separate Copy. 1877.
    The Pycnogonids, dredged during the Cruises of the Willem Barents in the years 1878 and 1879.
        Niederl. Arch. f. Zool. Supplementb. 1. p. 1—18 (Separate Copy). Pl. I—II. 1881.
— Report on the Pycnogonida.
        The Zool. of the Voy. of H. M. S. Challenger. Part. X. 1881.
    Nouvelles études sur les Pycnogonides.
        Arch. d. Zool. expér. et génér. Vol. IX. p. 445—542. Pl. XVIII—XXX. 1881.
Ihle, J. E. W.: Ueber die Phylogenie und systematische Stellung der Pantopoden.
        Biolog. Centralbl. XVIII. B. Nr. 16. 1898.
Jarzynsky, Th.: Praemissus catalogus Pycnogonidarum inventarum in mari glaciali ad oras Lap-
    poniae rossicae et in mari albo, anno 1869 et 70.
        Ann. d. l. soc. d. Natur. d. St. Pétersbourg. 1870.
Kingsley, J. S.: The Classification of the Arthropods.
        Amer. Natural. XXVIII. Febr. p. 118—35 and 220—35. 1894.
Korschelt, E. und Heider, K.: Lehrbuch der vergleichenden Entwicklungsgeschichte der wirbel-
    losen Thiere. Specieller Theil. Erstes Heft. 1890.
Kroyer, H.: Gronlands Amfipoder beskrevne. (Som Tillæg: Beskrivelse af nogle andre gronlandske
    Kræbsdyr, og Optælling af Kræbsdyrklassens hidtil bekjendte gronlandske Arter, i Forbindelse
    med nogle zoologisk-geografiske Bemærkninger over de boreale Krustaceer).
        K. D. Vid. Selsk. Nat. Math. Afhandl. VII. p. 229—326. Tab. I—IV. 1838.
— Om Pycnogonidernes Forvandlinger.
        Naturh. Tidsskr. 1. R. 3. B. p. 299—306. Pl. III. 1840.
— Bidrag til Kundskab om Pycnogoniderne eller Sospindlerne.
        Naturh. Tidsskr. 2. R. 1. B. p. 90—139. Pl. I. 1844.
— Gaimard, Voyages en Scandinavie, en Lapponie etc. Zoologie. Crustacées.
        Pl. 35—39. 1849.
Latreille, P. A.: Cuvier, Le règne animal, éd. II. Tome IV. 1829.
Locy, Wm.: Observations on the Development of Agelena naevia.
        Bull. Mus. Comp. Zoöl. Harv. Coll. Cambridge. Vol. XII. p. 63—103. Pl. I—XII. 1885.
Meinert, Fr.: Fluernes Munddele. Trophi Dipterorum. 1881.
Miers, Edw.: On a small Collection of Crustacea and Pycnogonida from Franz-Joseph Land, collected
    by B. Leigh Smith, Esq.
        The Ann. and Mag. of Natur. Hist. Ser. 5. Vol. VII. p. 45—51. Pl. VII. 1881.

Morgan, T. H.: A Contribution to the Embryology and Phylogeny of the Pycnogonids.
  Stud. from the Biolog. Laborat. Baltimore. Vol. V. Nr. 1. p. 1—76. Pl. I—VIII. 1891.

Sabine: Marine invertebrate animals.
  A Suppl. to the Append. of Capt. Parry's Voyage in the years 1819—20. 1824.

Sars, G. O.: Prodromus descriptionis Crustaceorum et Pycnogonidarum, quæ in Expeditione Norve-
  gica anno 1876 observavit.
  Arch. f. Math. og Naturv. II. p. 337—271 (371). 1877.

  Crustacea et Pycnogonida nova in itinere 2do et 3tio expeditionis Norvegicæ anno 1877 & 78
  collecta. (Prodromus descriptionis).
  Arch. f. Math. og Naturv. IV. p. 127—76. 1880.

  Pycnogonidea borealia & arctica enumerat (Prodromus descriptionis).
  Arch. f. Math. og Naturv. XII. p. 339—56. 1888.

  Pycnogonidea.
  Den norske Nordhavs-Expedition 1876—78. XX. Zoologi. Pl. I—XV. 1891.

Schimkewitsch, W.: Sur les Pantopodes recueillis par M. le lieutenant G. Chierchia pendant le
  voyage de la corvette Vettor Pisani en 1882—1885.
  Reale accad. dei Lincei (Anno CCLXXXVI 1889). Ser. 4. Mem. d. Cl. di sc. fis. mat. e nat.
  Vol. VI. 1890.

  Compte-rendu sur les Pantopodes.
  Rep. dredg. oper. of the West-Coast of Central-Amerika to the Galapagos etc. Bull. Mus. Comp.
  Zoöl. Harv. Coll. Vol. XXV. Nr. 2. p. 27—48. Pl. I—II. 1893.

Semper, C.: Ueber Pycnogoniden und ihre in Hydroiden schmarotzenden Larvenformen.
  Arbeiten aus d. Zool. Zoot. Instit. in Würzburg. I. p. 264—86. Taf. 16—17. 1874.

Wilson, Edm.: A Synopsis of the Pycnogonida of New England.
  Trans. Conn. Acad. of Arts and Sciences. V. Aug. 1878. p. 1—26. Pl. I—VII. 1878.
  The Pycnogonida of New England and Adjacent Waters.
  Rep. Unit. Stat. Commiss. of Fish and Fisheries. Part. VI. for 1878. p. 463—506. Pl. I—VII. 1878.
  Report on the Pycnogonida (Blake).
  Rep. Results Dredg. Superv. A. Agassiz, along the East Coast of Unit. Stat. etc. Bull. Mus.
  Comp. Zoöl. Harv. Coll. Vol. VIII. Nr. 12. p. 239—56. Pl. I—V. 1881.

Zenker: Untersuchungen über die Pycnogoniden.
  Arch. f. Anat. u. Phys. u. wiss. Medic. Jahrg. 1852. p. 379—91. Taf. X. 1852.

EXPLANATION OF THE PLATES.

Tab. I.

Fig. 1—4. *Pycnogonum littorale* Strøm.

Fig. 1: First beginning of the embryo, from below.
The proboscis and the three pairs of embryonal limbs are seen as low tubercles.

— 2: The embryo, somewhat more advanced, from below.
The embryonal legs are seen as long appendages, all resembling each other, with the only exception that the foremost pair show at the point an indistinct cleaving as the beginning of the fingers of the chela or hand.

— 3: Larva of the first stage, from below.

— 4: Larva of the third stage, dorsal view.
The embryonal limbs have all been thrown off, but the eyes are distinctly seen on the foremost, somewhat constricted part of the first segment of the trunk, and the three foremost pairs of the ambulatory legs have all their complete number of joints.

Fig. 5—6. *Phoxichilidium femoratum* Rathke.

Fig. 5: Larva of the first stage, from below.
The proboscis is not distinctly marked off, but seems to be a continuation of the trunk; byssus-threads wanting.

— 6: The same, dorsal view.
The outermost joints of the embryonal limbs have been cut off.

Fig. 7—9. *Pseudopallene spinipes* Fabr.

Fig. 7: Larva of the second stage inside the egg, lateral view.
Very early stage of development. No trace of embryonal legs.
a. Chelifori; *b*. foremost pair of ambulatory legs.

— 8: The same stage, lateral view.
Somewhat more advanced; in this specimen the rudimentary embryonal legs are seen.
a. First pair of embryonal legs; *b*. second pair of embryonal legs.

— 9: Free larva of the second stage, lateral view.
Here (only in this specimen?) no trace of embryonal legs are seen. The byssus-threads are now found.

Fig. 10—15. *Pseudopallene circularis* Goods.

Fig. 10: Free larva of the second stage, lateral view.
a. First pair of embryonal legs; *b*. second pair of embryonal legs; *c*. the byssus-gland.

Fig. 11: The same, from below.
. The common ganglionic mass.
12: Larva of the second stage, from below.
Here and in the following three figures only a small part of the ambulatory legs has been given.
13: The same, dorsal view.
14: Larva of the second stage, from below.
15: A young one, from below.
  t. t. Newly begun ovigerous legs.

Fig. 16—17. *Pallene brevirostris* Johnst.

Fig. 16: Free larva of the first stage, lateral view.
  a. First pair of embryonal legs; *b.* second pair of embryonal legs; *c.* byssus-threads.
17: The same, somewhat reduced, dorsal view.
  a. a. The byssus-threads from both the chelifori.

Fig. 18—19. *Pallene hastata* n. sp.

Fig. 18: Free larva of the second stage, lateral view.
  No trace of embryonal legs are seen here, such as in *Pall. brevirostris*, but the development is here somewhat more advanced, which may perhaps account for the difference.
  a. The proboscis.
 — 19: Free larva of the second stage, lateral view.
  The larval stage is here more advanced, near its close.
  t. The proboscis.

Fig. 20—29. *Nymphon grossipes* Fabr.

Fig. 20: Larva of the second stage, lateral view.
  The ambulatory legs begin to appear, and a byssus-thread is secreted.
21: Larva of the second stage, lateral view.
  The stage considerably more advanced.
22: The fore part of the same, more enlarged.
  a. Byssus-gland.
23: Larva of the second stage, dorsal view.
  The two foremost pairs of ambulatory legs are fully articulated with well developed claws and auxiliary claws, the second pair only want one joint.
  a. a. The byssus-glands.
24: The same, from below.
  The greater part of the two foremost pairs of ambulatory legs has been cut away. The yolk-mass is seen to continue from the trunk into the ambulatory legs, bordered by the future wall of the stomach.
  t. t. The byssus-glands; *b. b.* first pair of embryonal legs; *c. c.* second pair of embryonal legs.
25: The fore part of the same, more enlarged.
  t. The first embryonal leg; *b.* the second embryonal leg; *c.* the proboscis.
26: Larva of the third stage, dorsal view.
  The development of the fourth pair of ambulatory legs is already pretty well advanced.

PYCNOGONIDA. 67

Fig. 27: The same, from below.
The embryonal legs have now been thrown off, and the development of the imaginal fore
limbs has begun.
a. a. The palps; *b. b.* the ovigerous legs.
 — 28: A palp (third larval stage) newly begun.
 — 29: An ovigerous leg (third larval stage) newly begun.

Tab. II.

Fig. 1—7. *Nymphon robustum* Bell.

Fig. 1: First beginning of the embryo, lateral view.
The embryonal legs are seen as distinct swellings.
 — 2: Larva of the second stage, lateral view.
The larva is still enclosed in its membranes (and egg-shell?), but the trunk is already segmented, and the foremost pair of ambulatory legs are pretty long.
a. The chelifori; *b.* the first embryonal leg enclosed by a dermal sheath; *c.* the second embryonal leg; *d.* the proboscis; *e.* the first pair of ambulatory legs.
 3: The proboscis, somewhat more enlarged, lateral view.
Four cast-off sloughs of the proboscis are seen to be lying one within the other, with the
corresponding walls of the intestinal canal arranged in the same way.
 — 4: Larva of the second stage, lateral view.
This phase is older than that of fig. 2 it having got the byssus-threads; the second pair of
ambulatory legs are also long, and the first pair distinctly articulated; on the other hand
only the two foremost segments of the trunk have been constricted, and the two hindmost
pairs of ambulatory legs scarcely begun.
f. The second ambulatory leg. The other letters as in fig. 2.
 — 5: Free larva of the second stage, lateral view.
A still older phase than fig. 4: nevertheless the last pair of ambulatory legs have not yet
been fully developed, but the larva is free of the egg-shell and the membranes.
 6: The same, from below.
The letters as in the preceding figures.
 — 7: Larva of the third stage, dorsal view.
The embryonal legs and the byssus-threads are thrown off, but the newly begun imaginal
fore limbs have appeared. Of the ambulatory legs only one leg of the foremost pair has
been kept.
a. a. The chelifori; *b. b.* the palps; *c. c.* the beginning of the ovigerous legs.

Fig. 8—12. *Nymphon macronyx* G. O. Sars.

Fig. 8: Larva of the first stage, dorsal view.
The embryonal legs and the proboscis are hidden by the trunk.
a. a. The chelifori; *a.' a'.* the ducts of the byssus-glands.
 — 9: The same, from below.
a. a. The chelifori; *a'. a'.* the ducts of the byssus-glands; *b. b.* the first pair of embryonal legs;
c. c. the second pair of embryonal legs; *d.* the proboscis; *e.* common ganglionic mass for the
embryonal legs.

9*

1   The same, lateral view

The chelifonus; *a'*. duct of the byssus-gland; *b*. the first embryonal leg; *c*. the second embryonal leg; *d*. the proboscis; *c*. the byssus-gland.

11: Larva of the second stage, lateral view.

c. The three foremost ambulatory legs. The other letters as in the preceding figure.

12: Larva of the second stage, lateral view.

An older phase than fig. 11.

c. Chelifonus; *b*. the first embryonal leg; *c*. the second embryonal leg; *d*. the proboscis; *c*. the first ambulatory leg; *f*. the second ambulatory leg.

Fig. 13—14. *Nymphon spinosum* Goods.

Fig. 13: Larva of the second stage, lateral view.

The larva is in a very early phase of the second stage, still lying in the egg-shell, and with the foremost pair of ambulatory legs only short and still unjointed.

a. Chelifonus; *a'*. duct of the byssus-gland; *b*. the first embryonal leg; *c*. the second embryonal leg; *d*. the first ambulatory leg; *c*. byssus-gland; *f*. egg-shell.

14: Larva of the third stage, from below.

The embryonal legs and the byssus-threads have fallen off, but the articulation of the imaginal fore limbs has begun. Of the fully developed ambulatory legs only one leg of the second pair is kept.

a. a. The chelifori; *b. b.* the palps; *c. c.* the ovigerous legs.

Fig. 15—16. *Nymphon elegans* Hans.

Fig. 15: Free larva of the first stage, lateral view.

The beginning of the second stage is marked by the appearance of the byssus-threads. The letters as in fig. 13.

16: Larva of the second stage, lateral view.

a. Chelifonus; *a'*. duct of the byssus-gland; *b*. the first embryonal leg; *c*. the second embryonal leg; *d*. the proboscis; *c*. the first ambulatory leg; *f*. the second and third ambulatory leg; *g*. byssus-gland.

Fig. 17—18. *Nymphon Sluiteri* Hoek.

Fig. 17: Larva of the second stage, lateral view.

a. Chelifonus; *b*. the first embryonal leg; *c*. the second embryonal leg; *d*. the proboscis; *c*. the first ambulatory leg; *f*. the second ambulatory leg; *g*. beginning of the third ambulatory leg.

— 18: The same, from below.

Of the ambulatory legs only the basal end is kept.

a. a. The chelifori; *b. b.* the first pair of embryonal legs; *c. c.* the second pair of embryonal legs; *d*. the proboscis; *c*. the ganglionic mass for the embryonal legs; *f*. the ganglion of the first segment of trunk; *g*. the whole ganglionic mass for the rest of the trunk.

Fig. 19—21. *Nymphon longitarse* K1.

Fig. 19: Larva of the first stage, dorsal view.

a. a. The chelifori; *a'. a'.* the ducts of the byssus-glands; *b. b.* the first pair of embryonal legs; the second pair of embryonal legs; *d. d.* the byssus-glands.

Fig. 20: The same, from below.

d. The proboscis; e. ganglionic mass for the embryonal legs. The other letters as in the preceding figure.

— 21: The same, lateral view.

The letters as in fig. 19.

Fig. 22—24. *Paranymphon spinipes* Caull.[1])

Fig. 22: Larva of the first stage, dorsal view.

The letters as in fig. 20.

23: The same, from below.

The letters as in fig. 20.

24: The same, lateral view.

By a pressure of the covering glass the yolk-mass has been forced out into the first joint of the right cheliforus, and has distended this joint; the claws of the embryonal legs have also been curved by the same pressure.

Fig. 25— 27. *Zetes hispidus* Kr.

Fig. 25: Larva of the first stage, in the egg-shell, lateral view.

a. Cheliforus; b. the first embryonal leg; c. the second embryonal leg; d. the proboscis; e. egg-shell.

— 26: Fore end of the same, more enlarged, lateral view.

a. Cheliforus; a'. duct of the byssus-gland; b. first embryonal leg; c. second embryonal leg; d. proboscis; e. egg-shell.

— 27: Larva of the first stage, dorsal view.

The letters as in the preceding figure.

Tab. III.

Fig. 1—6. *Nymphon Sarsii* n. sp.

Fig. 1: Full figure, dorsal view. 3 times enlarged.

— 2: The same, lateral view; all limbs removed. 6 times enlarged.

— 3: A cheliforus.

— 4: The outermost joints of the palps.

— 5: The outermost joints of the ovigerous legs.

- 6: The two joints of the foot with claw and auxiliary claws.

Fig. 7—13. *Nymphon Hoekii* n. sp.

Fig. 7: Full figure, dorsal view. 3 times enlarged.

- 8: The same, lateral view; all limbs removed. 6 times enlarged.

— 9: A cheliforus.

— 10: The outermost joints of the palps.

11: The outermost joints of the ovigerous legs.

— 12: The claw of the ovigerous legs.

— 13: The two joints of the foot with claw and auxiliary claws.

[1]) The specific name of *spinipes* here in this plate is an error for *spinosum*.

PYCNOGONIDA

Fig. 14—22. *Nymphon Groenlandicum* n. sp.

Fig. 14 Full figure, dorsal view. 3 times enlarged.
  15: The same, lateral view; all limbs removed. 6 times enlarged.
  16: Oculiferous tubercle, from behind.
  17: A cheliforus.
  18: The ends of the fingers of the chela.
  19: The outermost joints of the palps.
  20: An ovigerous leg. *a.* sensory (?).
  21: A dermal leaf from the terminal part of the ovigerous leg.
  22: The two joints of the foot with claw and auxiliary claws.

Fig. 23—24. *Nymphon robustum* Bell.

Fig. 23: The distal end of the fourth joint of the ovigerous legs.
  24: The proximal end of the fifth joint of the ovigerous legs.

Tab. IV.

Fig. 1—7. *Pallenopsis plumipes* n. sp.

Fig. 1: Full figure, dorsal view. Natural size.
  a. a. The rudimentary palps.
  2: The same, lateral view; all limbs removed. Natural size.
  a. Palp.
  3: Fore end of the first segment of trunk with oculiferous tubercle and part of the chelifori. Below the oculiferous tubercle with the two foremost eyes the metamere of the chelifori is seen; the first joints of the chelifori are truncate.
  4: Outermost joint of the chelifori.
  5: An ovigerous leg.
  6: The outermost joint of an ovigerous leg.
  7: The outermost joints of an ambulatory leg.

Fig. 8—13. *Pallene acus* n. sp.

Fig. 8: Full figure, dorsal view. 5 times enlarged.
  9: The same, lateral view; all limbs removed. 10 times enlarged.
  10: The chela of a cheliforus.
  11: The outermost joints of an ovigerous leg.
  12: Three dermal leaves of the terminal part of an ovigerous leg.
  13: The outermost joints of an ambulatory leg, with the edge on the last joint.

Fig. 14—19. *Pallene hastata* n. sp.

Fig. 14: Full figure, dorsal view. 6 times enlarged.
  15: The same, lateral view; all limbs removed. 12 times enlarged.
  16: The chela of a cheliforus.
  17: An ovigerous leg, with distinct sensory (?).
  a. Sensory (?).
  18: The outermost joints of an ambulatory leg, with the edge on the last joint.
  19: Part of the same edge, with a couple of the thorns of the leg. Much enlarged.

Fig. 20—28. *Paranymphon spinosum* Caull.

Fig. 20: Full figure, dorsal view. 6 times enlarged.
— 21: The same, lateral view; all limbs removed. 12 times enlarged.
— 22: A cheliforus with the chela bent backward.
— 23: The movable finger of the chela.
— 24: The outermost joints of a palp.
— 25: An ovigerous leg.
— 26: The outermost joints of an ovigerous leg.
— 27: An ambulatory leg.
— 28: The outermost joints of an ambulatory leg. More enlarged.

Tab. V.

Fig. 1—6. *Pallenopsis fluminensis* Kr.

Fig. 1: Full figure, dorsal view. 3 times enlarged.
On account of the position of the animal the gland ducts on the ambulatory legs are not seen in this figure.
— 2: The same, lateral view; all limbs removed. 6 times enlarged.
— 3: A cheliforus.
— 4: An ovigerous leg.
— 5: Part of the fourth joint of the first pair of ambulatory legs of the male, with gland duct.
— 6: The outermost joints of an ambulatory leg with claws and auxiliary claws.

Fig. 7—18. *Ascorhynchus tridens* n. sp.

Fig. 7: Full figure, lateral view; all limbs removed. 6 times enlarged.
— 8: The same, lateral view; all limbs removed. 8 times enlarged.
— 9: Oculiferous tubercle, from behind.
— 10: The outermost joints of a cheliforus (in a full-grown animal).
— 11: A cheliforus of a very young animal.
— 12: A cheliforus of a somewhat older animal.
— 13: A cheliforus of a full-grown animal (abnormal).
— 14: A palp with distinct sensory (?).
a. Sensory (?).
— 15: An ovigerous leg.
— 16: A dermal leaf from the terminal part of the ovigerous leg.
— 17: The outermost joints of an ambulatory leg, in the male.
— 18: The outermost joints of an ambulatory leg, in the female.

Fig. 19—20. *Colossendeis clavata* n. sp.

Fig. 19: Full figure, dorsal view. Two thirds of the natural size.
— 20: The same, lateral view; all limbs removed. Twice the natural size.

Fig. 21—22. *Colossendeis angusta* G. O. Sars.

Fig. 21: A cheliforus of a very young animal.
— 22: The outermost joints of a palp of a very young animal.

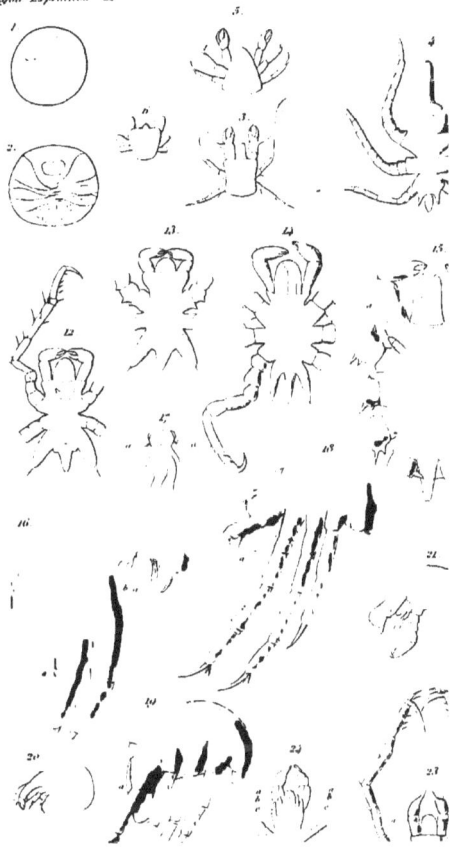

Nymphon robustum 1 7.   Nymph. macronyx 8 12.   Nymph. spinosum 13 14.   Nymph. elegans. 15 16.
Nymph. Sluiteri 17 18.   Nymph. longitarse 19 21.   Paranymphon spinipes 22 24.   Zetes hispidus 25 27.

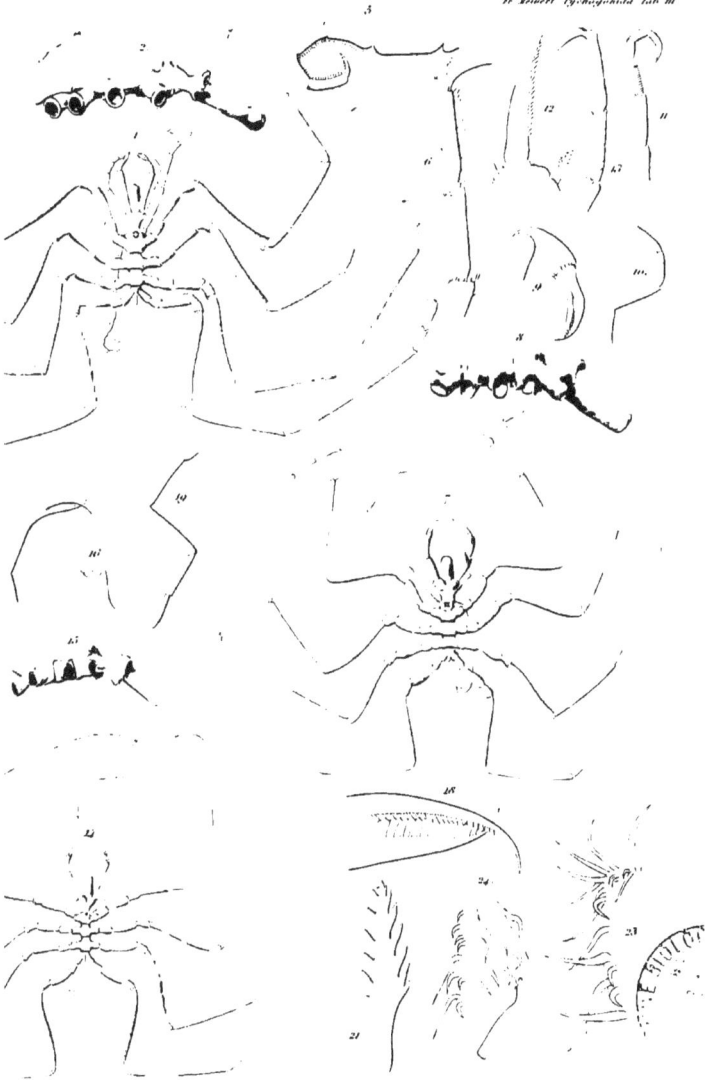

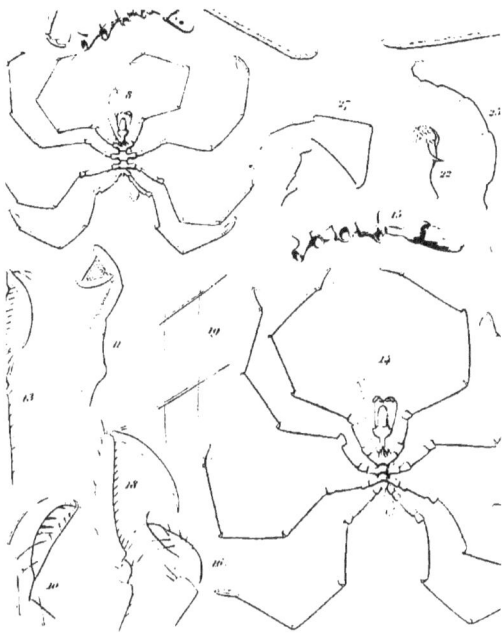

Pallenopsis plumipes 1 7   *Pallene acus* 8 15   1
Paranymphon spinosum 20 28

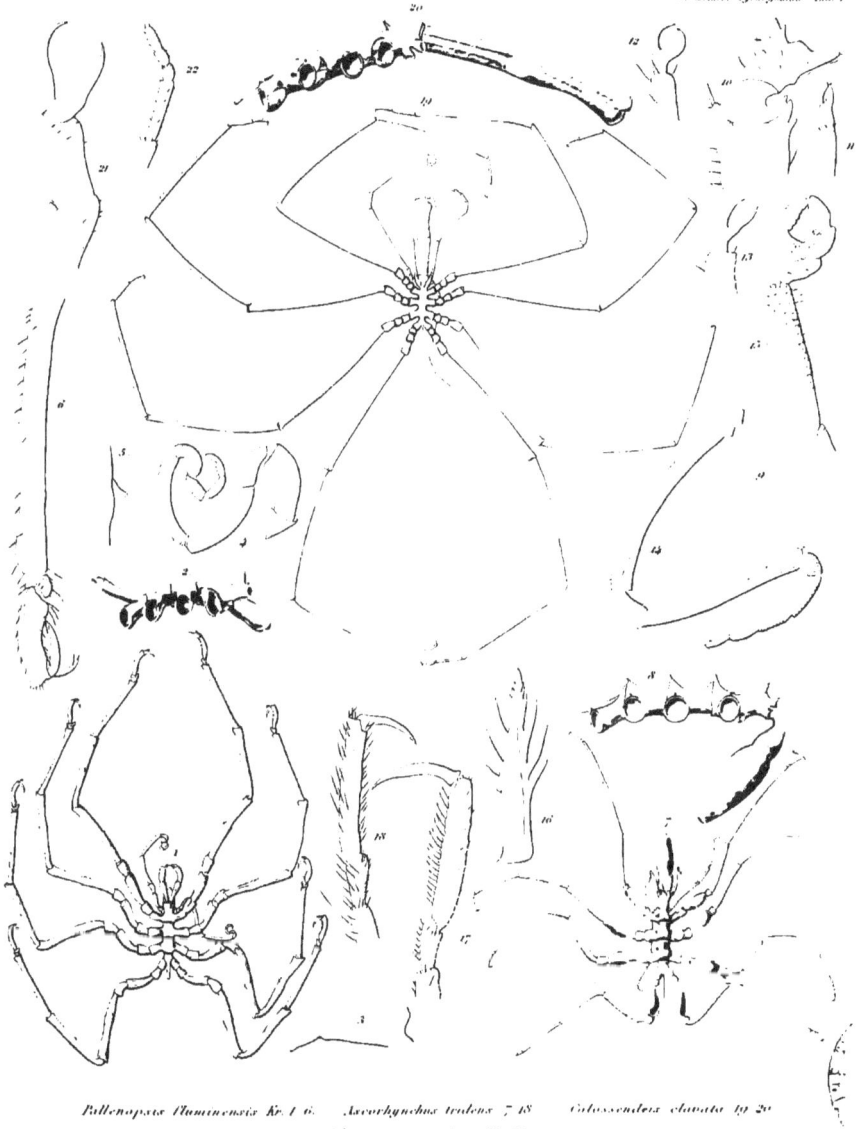

Pallenopsis flaminensis Kr. 1. 6. Ascorhynchus tridens 7. 18. Colossendeis clavata 19. 20.
Coloss angusta jun. 21. 22.

THE INGOLF-EXPEDITION

1895—1896.

THE LOCALITIES, DEPTHS, AND BOTTOMTEMPERATURES OF THE STATIONS.

Station Nr.	Lat. N.	Long. W.	Depth in Danish fathoms	Bottom-temp.	Station Nr.	Lat. N.	Long. W.	Depth in Danish fathoms	Bottom-temp.	Station Nr.	Lat. N.	Long. W.	Depth in Danish fathoms	Bottom-temp.
1	62° 30'	8° 21'	132	7°2	24	63° 06'	56° 00'	1199	2°1	45	61° 32'	9° 43'	643	4°17
2	63° 04'	9° 22'	262	5°3	25	63° 30'	54° 25'	582	3°3	46	61° 32'	11° 36'	720	2°40
3	63° 35'	10° 21'	272	0°5		63° 51'	53° 03'	136		47	61° 32'	13° 40'	950	3°23
4	61° 07'	11° 12'	237	2°5	26	63° 57'	52° 41'	34	0°6	48	61° 32'	15° 11'	1150	3°17
5	64° 40'	12° 09'	155			64° 37'	54° 24'	109		49	62° 07'	15° 07'	1120	2°91
6	63° 43'	14° 34'	90	7°0	27	64° 54'	55° 10'	393	3°8	50	62° 43'	15° 07'	1020	3°13
7	63° 13'	15° 41'	600	4°5	28	65° 14'	55° 42'	420	305	51	64° 15'	14° 22'	68	7°32
8	63° 56'	24° 40'	136	6°0	29	65° 34'	54° 31'	68	0°2	52	63° 57'	13° 32'	420	7°87
9	64° 18'	27° 00'	295	5°8	30	66° 50'	54° 28'	22	1°05	53	63° 15'	13° 07'	795	3°68
10	64° 24'	28° 50'	788	3°5	31	66° 35'	55° 54'	88	1°6	54	63° 08'	15° 40'	691	3°9
11	64° 34'	31° 12'	1300	1°6	32	66° 35'	56° 38'	318	3°9	55	63° 33'	15° 02'	316	5°9
12	64° 38'	32° 37'	1040	0°3	33	67° 57'	55° 30'	35	0°8	56	64° 00'	15° 09'	68	7°57
13	64° 47'	34° 33'	622	3°0	34	65° 17'	54° 17'	55		57	63° 37'	13° 02'	350	3°4
14	64° 45'	35° 05'	176	4°4	35	65° 16'	55° 05'	362	3°6	58	64° 25'	12° 09'	211	0°8
15	66° 18'	25° 59'	330	-0°75	36	61° 50'	56° 21'	1435	1°5	59	65° 00'	11° 16'	310	0°1
16	65° 43'	26° 58'	250	6°1	37	60° 17'	54° 05'	1715	1°4	60	65° 09'	12° 27'	124	0°9
17	62° 49'	26° 55'	745	3°4	38	59° 12'	51° 05'	1870	1°3	61	65° 03'	13° 06'	55	0°4
18	61° 44'	30° 29'	1135	3°0	39	62° 00'	22° 38'	865	2°9	62	63° 18'	19° 12'	72	7°92
19	60° 29'	34° 14'	1566	2°4	40	62° 00'	21° 36'	845	3°3	63	62° 40'	19° 05'	800	4°0
20	58° 20'	40° 48'	1695	1°5	41	61° 39'	17° 10'	1245	2°0	64	62° 06'	19° 00'	1041	3°1
21	58° 01'	44° 45'	1330	2°4	42	61° 41'	16° 17'	625	0°4	65	61° 33'	19° 00'	1089	3°0
22	58° 10'	48° 25'	1845	1°4	43	61° 42'	16° 11'	645	0°05	66	61° 33'	20° 43'	1128	3°3
23	60° 43'	56° 00'	Only the Plankton Net used		44	61° 42'	9° 36'	515	4°8	67	61° 30'	22° 30'	975	3°0

Station Nr.	Long. W.	Lat. N	Depth in Danish fathoms	Bottom-temp.
68	62° 06'	22° 30'	843	3°4
69	62° 40'	22° 17'	589	3°9
70	63° 09'	22° 05'	134	7°0
71	63° 46'	22° 03'	46	
72	63° 12'	23° 04'	197	6°7
73	62° 58'	23° 28'	486	5°5
74	62° 17'	24° 36'	695	4°2
	61° 57'	25° 35'	761	
	61° 28'	25° 06'	829	
75	61° 28'	26° 25'	780	4°3
76	61° 50'	26° 50'	846	4°1
77	61° 10'	26° 59'	951	3°6
78	60° 37'	27° 32'	799	4°5
79	60° 52'	28° 58'	653	4°4
80	61° 02'	29° 32'	935	4°0
81	61° 44'	27° 00'	485	6°1
82	61° 55'	27° 28'	824	4°1
83	62° 25'	28° 30'	912	3°5
	62° 36'	26° 01'	472	
	62° 36'	25° 30'	401	
84	62° 58'	25° 24'	633	4°8
85	63° 21'	25° 21'	170	
86	65° 03'	23° 47'	76	
87	65° 02'	23° 56'	110	
88	64° 58'	24° 15'	76	6°9
89	64° 45'	27° 20'	310	8°4
90	64° 45'	29° 06'	568	4°4
91	64° 44'	31° 00'	1236	3°1

Station Nr.	Lat. N	Long. W.	Depth in Danish fathoms	Bottom-temp.
92	64° 44'	32° 52'	976	1°4
93	64° 24'	35° 14'	767	1°46
94	64° 56'	36° 19'	204	4°1
	65° 31'	30° 45'	213	
95	65° 14'	30° 39'	752	2°1
96	65° 21'	29° 00'	735	1°2
97	65° 28'	27° 39'	450	5°5
98	65° 38'	26° 27'	138	5°9
99	66° 13'	25° 53'	187	6°1
100	66° 23'	14° 02'	59	0°4
101	66° 23'	12° 05'	537	0°7
102	66° 23'	10° 26'	750	0°9
103	66° 23'	8° 52'	579	0°6
104	66° 23'	7° 25'	957	−1°1
105	65° 34'	7° 31'	762	0°8
106	65° 34'	8° 54'	447	−0°6
	65° 29'	8° 40'	466	
107	63° 33'	10° 28'	492	−0°3
108	65° 30'	12° 00'	97	1°1
109	65° 29'	13° 25'	38	1°5
110	66° 44'	11° 33'	781	0°8
111	67° 14'	8° 48'	860	−0°9
112	67° 57'	6° 44'	1267	−1°1
113	69° 31'	7° 06'	1309	1°0
114	70° 36'	7° 29'	773	1°0
115	70° 50'	8° 29'	86	0°1
116	70° 05'	8° 26'	371	0°4
117	69° 13'	8° 23'	1003	1°0

Station Nr.	Lat. N.	Long. W.	Depth in Danish fathoms	Bottom-temp.
118	68° 27'	8° 20'	1060	1°0
119	67° 53'	10° 19'	1010	1°0
120	67° 29'	11° 32'	885	1°0
121	66° 59'	13° 11'	529	0°7
122	66° 42'	14° 44'	115	1°8
123	66° 52'	15° 40'	145	2°0
124	67° 40'	15° 40'	495	−0°6
125	68° 08'	16° 02'	729	−0°8
126	67° 19'	15° 52'	293	0°5
127	66° 33'	20° 05'	44	5°6
128	66° 50'	20° 02'	194	0°6
129	66° 35'	23° 47'	117	6°5
130	63° 00'	20° 40'	338	6°55
131	63° 00'	19° 09'	698	4°7
132	63° 00'	17° 04'	747	4°6
133	63° 14'	11° 24'	230	2°2
134	62° 34'	10° 26'	299	4°1
135	62° 48'	9° 48'	270	0°4
136	63° 01'	9° 11'	256	4°8
137	63° 14'	8° 31'	297	−0°6
138	63° 26'	7° 56'	471	0°6
139	63° 36'	7° 30'	702	0°6
140	63° 29'	6° 57'	780	−0°9
141	63° 22'	6° 58'	679	0°6
142	63° 07'	7° 05'	587	−0°6
143	62° 58'	7° 09'	388	−0°1
144	62° 49'	7° 12'	276	1°6

>-○-◆-◆-○-←

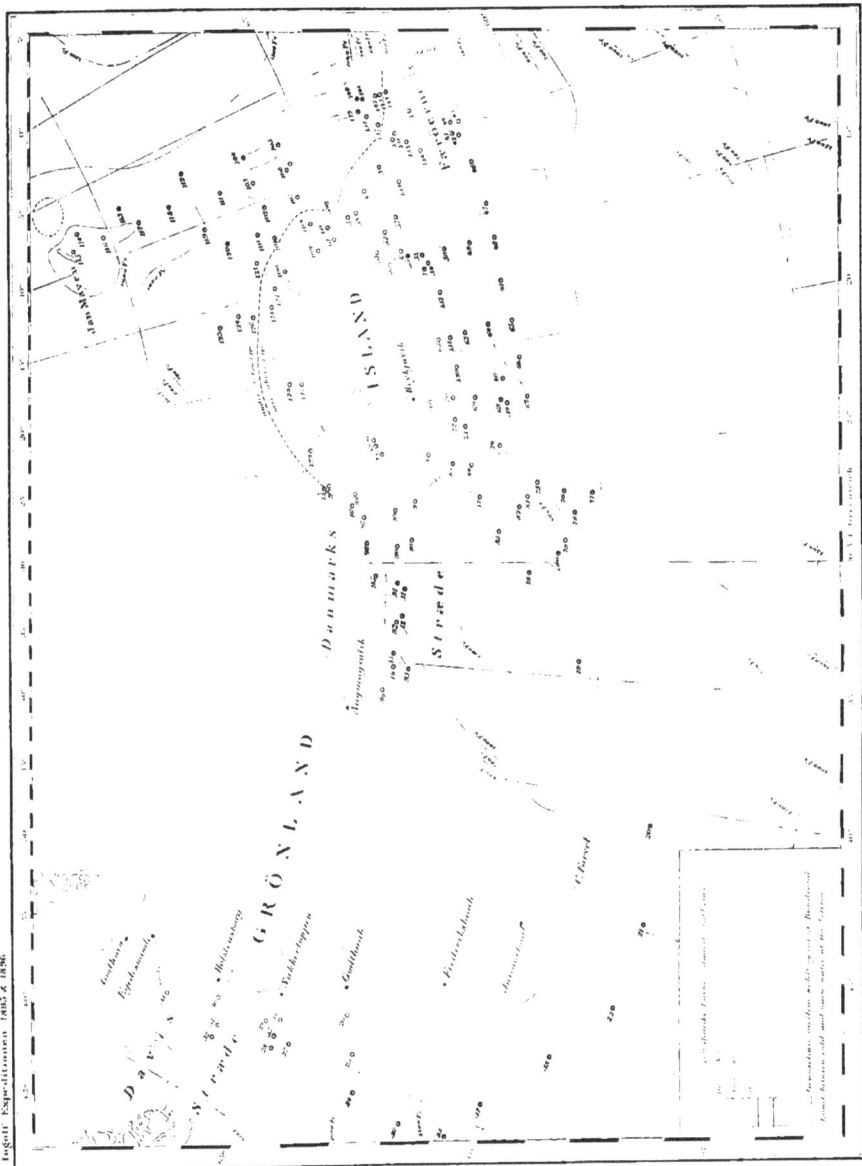

www.ingramcontent.com/pod-product-compliance
Lightning Source LLC
Chambersburg PA
CBHW021417090426
42742CB00009B/1173